GREAT JOBS

Er...ng

Mc Graw Hill

New York   Chicago   San Francisco   Lisbon   London   Madrid   Mexico City
Milan   New Delhi   San Juan   Seoul   Singapore   Sydney   Toronto

Library of Congress Cataloging-in-Publication Data

Garner, Geraldine O.
    Great jobs for engineering majors / by Geraldine O. Garner. — 3rd ed.
        p.   cm.
    Includes bibliographical references and index.
    ISBN 0-07-149314-X (alk. paper)
    1. Engineering—Vocational guidance.   I. Title.

    TA157.G327   2008
    620.0023—dc22   2007047009

1 2 3 4 5 6 7 8 9 10 11 12 13 14 15 16 17 18 19 20 21 22 23 24   DOC/DOC   0 9 8

ISBN 978-0-07-149314-7
MHID   0-07-149314-X

McGraw-Hill books are available at special quantity discounts to use as premiums and sales promotions or for use in corporate training programs. To contact a representative, please visit the Contact Us pages at www.mhprofessional.com.

This book is printed on acid-free paper.

This book is dedicated to the Virginia Tech engineering students and faculty who were victims of the April 16, 2007, tragedy. Royalties from this book will go to the Virginia Tech College of Engineering General Scholarship Fund in their memory.

Contents

Acknowledgments

It has been my privilege to know many engineering students who participated in the Cooperative Engineering Education (Co-op) Programs at Virginia Tech and Northwestern University. They made and implemented decisions about their engineering careers early in their college experience. Many took risks to pursue their goals and all experienced the rich diversity that the field of engineering has to offer. Each one had a unique story but they all possessed a seriousness of purpose and a commitment to their own development.

It continues to be personally rewarding to learn of their professional successes in the field. Some have become leaders of industry and others will take their place as leaders in the years to come.

Special thanks must also go to engineering Co-op employers, both large and small. This is a very special group of employers. They recognize the value of participating in the engineering education of successive generations of engineering students. They do so by providing supervision and guidance, as well as progressive levels of experience that transform students into engineers. Their individual interest in and personal concern for each student is quite incredible to observe.

This edition would not be possible without the contributions of David Siegel of the National Society of Professional Engineers; Thomas Moriarty of Norton Abbott Analysis, Ltd.; John Fabijanic of California State University, San Luis Obispo; and Steve Jahnke of Texas Instruments.

As always, the generosity, patience, support, and love of Jerry, Lauren, John, Adrian, Richelle, Avery, and Riley make everything worthwhile!

Introduction

Engineering: A Degree for the Twenty-First Century

If you are reading this book, you have probably chosen engineering as your college major. You may have also selected a specific engineering discipline. While your concentration, specialization, or minor in engineering will further define your interests, you probably still have questions such as "What can I do with my degree?" "What are the career paths that I can follow?" and "How do I get there from here?"

While others may be saying "you have it made," "you can write your own ticket," and "the employers are only interested in engineers!," you may feel some degree of frustration, even bewilderment, about how to manage your career. Unfortunately, engineers do not always receive the special guidance and advice needed to make the transition from engineering student to engineering professional.

This phenomenon tends to happen for two major reasons. First, there is a popular myth that engineers have it made in the job market. After all, the majority of employers coming to the career services office are looking for engineers. Second, because most employers who come to career services are looking for engineers, these offices must give attention to those in majors that are less often recruited. Unfortunately, when it comes to job search techniques and career planning, one size does not fit all, especially for engineers!

Techniques developed to assist liberal arts majors are not always appropriate for engineers. For example, liberal arts majors have the challenge of convincing employers that they possess generalized skills, such as organizational ability, the ability to work under pressure, communication skills, and so forth. On the other hand, engineers must quickly document and demonstrate that they have specific technical skills demanded by their field and/or the positions for which they apply. For example, engineering majors must document and demonstrate their knowledge of and experience in utilizing such things as statistical modeling or simulation software, computer-aided design programs, and up-to-date programming languages. For engineering majors, these skills are not up for speculation.

In addition, industry's increased reliance on résumé databases means that engineering managers are searching the database using "keywords" that are very objective. Managers typically enter criteria, such as the engineering major required, the specific software applications needed on the job, and the years of related experience in the field. Engineering candidates must make sure that these are well documented on the résumé or they will not come to the attention of the hiring managers.

Another difference is the career paths available to engineering majors. Liberal arts career paths tend to be amorphous and individual. By contrast, many engineering employers offer both specific and customized career paths for entry-level engineers. Consequently, engineering employers have different expectations of their job candidates. This book is designed to help you meet those expectations.

It has been said that "Spectacular achievements are always preceded by unspectacular preparation." As an engineering major, you know the true meaning of those words. Those nights in the lab! The unending problem sets! While the starting salaries and the number of offers might be "spectacular" to family and friends, it is the rigorous and time-intensive (unspectacular) preparation that actually provides the foundation for achievement in engineering.

Engineering majors such as those in civil, environmental, or biomedical engineering might not see as many employers recruiting on campus as those in other engineering disciplines. Their preparation process thus becomes even more important, because they will have to manage more of their own job search than some of their peers. For others, there will be many options from which to select. That may sound wonderful, but it is not always easy. Therefore, the same approach to preparation is important for both:

Know yourself.
Know the job market for your major.
Know the skills that you want to use on the job.
Know the quality of life you want to have.

Today, engineers are not just in the manufacturing facilities and government agencies. They are in medical school and law school. They work in banks and insurance companies. They teach and they consult in areas ranging from infrastructure and computer networking to business strategy. As an engineering major, your options are almost limitless and the choices can be challenging to make.

Nonetheless, it is worthwhile to prepare well to find your place in this myriad of opportunities. Although the preparation will take time and commitment on your part, the results should be rewarding. And, remember, at this early point in your career, there are very few decisions that you make that can't be undone and a new approach taken.

The best advice is to take it one step at a time. This book will begin by focusing on you. What are your goals, your interests, and your values? What are your personal strengths, and what are the technical skills that you have to offer?

As you progress through the book you will begin to focus on "what is out there." What is it? How do you prepare for it? And, what do you have to do to advance? As your self-knowledge and your knowledge of your field increases, you will begin to identify professional areas of interest for you. This will allow you to target those opportunities that are a good match for you at this point in time and that will provide the basis for your growth and development in the future.

Always keep in mind that the focus of this book is the career paths that are available to people who have majored in engineering. The paths are sufficiently broad in scope to provide great opportunities for you to find a good fit between your personal strengths, goals, and values and the environments in which engineers work. Career satisfaction is highly correlated to the fit between the person and the work environment, and career success is related, in part, to that satisfaction. So the process of finding the right fit is a very worthwhile one.

PART ONE

THE JOB SEARCH

1

The Self-Assessment

Self-assessment is the process by which you begin to acknowledge your own particular blend of education, experiences, values, needs, and goals. It provides the foundation for career planning and the entire job search process. Self-assessment involves looking inward and asking yourself what can sometimes prove to be difficult questions. This self-examination should lead to an intimate understanding of your personal traits and values, consumption patterns and economic needs, longer-term goals, skill base, preferred skills, and underdeveloped skills.

You come to the self-assessment process knowing yourself well in some of these areas, but you may still be uncertain about other aspects. You may be well aware of your consumption patterns, but have you spent much time specifically identifying your longer-term goals or your personal values as they relate to work? No matter what level of self-assessment you have undertaken to date, it is now time to clarify all of these issues and questions as they relate to the job search.

The knowledge you gain in the self-assessment process will guide the rest of your job search. In this book, you will learn about all of the following tasks:

- Writing résumés and cover letters
- Researching careers and networking
- Interviewing and job offer considerations

In each of these steps, you will rely on and often return to the understanding gained through your self-assessment. Any individual seeking employment must be able and willing to express these facets of his or her personality to recruiters and interviewers throughout the job search. This communication allows you to show the world who you are so that together with employers you can determine whether there will be a workable match with a given job or career path.

How to Conduct a Self-Assessment

The self-assessment process goes on naturally all the time. People ask you to clarify what you mean, you make a purchasing decision, or you begin a new relationship. You react to the world and the world reacts to you. How you understand these interactions and any changes you might make because of them are part of the natural process of self-discovery. There is, however, a more comprehensive and efficient way to approach self-assessment with regard to employment.

Because self-assessment can become a complex exercise, we have distilled it into a seven-step process that provides an effective basis for undertaking a job search. The seven steps include the following:

1. Understanding your personal traits
2. Identifying your personal values
3. Calculating your economic needs
4. Exploring your longer-term goals
5. Enumerating your skill base
6. Recognizing your preferred skills
7. Assessing skills needing further development

As you work through your self-assessment, you might want to create a worksheet similar to the one shown in Exhibit 1.1, starting on the following page. Or you might want to keep a journal of the thoughts you have as you undergo this process. There will be many opportunities to revise your self-assessment as you start down the path of seeking a career.

Step 1 Understand Your Personal Traits
Each person has a unique personality that he or she brings to the job search process. Gaining a better understanding of your personal traits can help you evaluate job and career choices. Identifying these traits and then finding employment that allows you to draw on at least some of them can create a rewarding and fulfilling work experience. If potential employment doesn't allow you to use these preferred traits, it is important to decide whether you

Exhibit 1.1
SELF-ASSESSMENT WORKSHEET

Step 1. Understand Your Personal Traits

The personal traits that describe me are
(Include all of the words that describe you.)
The ten personal traits that most accurately describe me are
(List these ten traits.)

Step 2. Identify Your Personal Values

Working conditions that are important to me include
(List working conditions that would have to exist for you to accept a position.)
The values that go along with my working conditions are
(Write down the values that correspond to each working condition.)
Some additional values I've decided to include are
(List those values you identify as you conduct this job search.)

Step 3. Calculate Your Economic Needs

My estimated minimum annual salary requirement is
(Write the salary you have calculated based on your budget.)
Starting salaries for the positions I'm considering are
(List the name of each job you are considering and the associated starting salary.)

Step 4. Explore Your Longer-Term Goals

My thoughts on longer-term goals right now are
(Jot down some of your longer-term goals as you know them right now.)

Step 5. Enumerate Your Skill Base

The general skills I possess are
(List the skills that underlie tasks you are able to complete.)
The specific skills I possess are
(List more technical or specific skills that you possess, and indicate your level of expertise.)
General and specific skills that I want to promote to employers for the jobs I'm considering are
(List general and specific skills for each type of job you are considering.)

continued

Step 6. Recognize Your Preferred Skills

Skills that I would like to use on the job include

(*List skills that you hope to use on the job, and indicate how often you'd like to use them.*)

Step 7. Assess Skills Needing Further Development

Some skills that I'll need to acquire for the jobs I'm considering include

(*Write down skills listed in job advertisements or job descriptions that you don't currently possess.*)

I believe I can build these skills by

(*Describe how you plan to acquire these skills.*)

can find other ways to express them or whether you would be better off not considering this type of job. Interests and hobbies pursued outside of work hours can be one way to use personal traits you don't have an opportunity to draw on in your work. For example, if you consider yourself an outgoing person and the kinds of jobs you are examining allow little contact with other people, you may be able to achieve the level of interaction that is comfortable for you outside of your work setting. If such a compromise seems impractical or otherwise unsatisfactory, you probably should explore only jobs that provide the interaction you want and need on the job.

Many young adults who are not very confident about their employability will downplay their need for income. They will say, "Money is not all that important if I love my work." But if you begin to document exactly what you need for housing, transportation, insurance, clothing, food, and utilities, you will begin to understand that some jobs cannot meet your financial needs and it doesn't matter how wonderful the job is. If you have to worry each payday about bills and other financial obligations, you won't be very effective on the job. Begin now to be honest with yourself about your needs.

Begin the self-assessment process by creating an inventory of your personal traits. Make a list of as many words as possible to describe yourself. Words like *accurate, creative, future-oriented, relaxed,* or *structured* are just a few examples. In addition, you might ask people who know you well how they might describe you.

Focus on Selected Personal Traits. Of all the traits you identified, select the ten you believe most accurately describe you. Keep track of these ten traits.

Consider Your Personal Traits in the Job Search Process. As you begin exploring jobs and careers, watch for matches between your personal traits and the job descriptions you read. Some jobs will require many personal traits you know you possess, and others will not seem to match those traits.

A researcher's work, for example, requires an attention to detail, self-discipline, motivation, curiosity, and observation. Researchers often work on the same project for an extended period of time and they tend to work alone or in a small group, with limited opportunities to interact with others. Professors, on the other hand, must interact regularly with students and colleagues to carry out their teaching program. Educators need strong interpersonal and verbal skills, imagination, and a good sense of humor. They must enjoy being in front of groups and must become skilled at presenting information using a variety of methods to appeal to various learning styles.

Your ability to respond to changing conditions, your decision-making ability, productivity, creativity, and verbal skills all have a bearing on your success in and enjoyment of your work life. To better guarantee success, be sure to take the time needed to understand these traits in yourself.

Step 2   Identify Your Personal Values

Your personal values affect every aspect of your life, including employment, and they develop and change as you move through life. Values can be defined as principles that we hold in high regard, qualities that are important and desirable to us. Some values aren't ordinarily connected to work (love, beauty, color, light, relationships, family, or religion), and others are (autonomy, cooperation, effectiveness, achievement, knowledge, and security). Our values determine, in part, the level of satisfaction we feel in a particular job.

Define Acceptable Working Conditions. One facet of employment is the set of working conditions that must exist for someone to consider taking a job.

Each of us would probably create a unique list of acceptable working conditions, but items that might be included on many people's lists are the amount of money you would need to be paid, how far you are willing to drive or travel, the amount of freedom you want in determining your own schedule, whether you would be working with people or data or things, and the types of tasks you would be willing to do. Your conditions might include statements of working conditions you will *not* accept; for example, you might not be willing to work at night or on weekends or holidays.

If you were offered a job tomorrow, what conditions would have to exist for you to realistically consider accepting the position? Take some time and make a list of these conditions.

Realize Associated Values. Your list of working conditions can be used to create an inventory of your values relating to jobs and careers you are exploring. For example, if one of your conditions stated that you wanted to earn at least $30,000 per year, the associated value would be financial gain. If another condition was that you wanted to work with a friendly group of people, the value that went along with that might be belonging or interaction with people.

Relate Your Values to the World of Work. As you read the job descriptions you come across either in this book, in newspapers and magazines, or online, think about the values associated with each position.

For example, civil engineers work on almost every facility that is essential to modern life, from smart highways to green buildings to high-tech transit systems and spacecraft. Associated values include community service, development, and improvement, as well as meeting the challenges of pollution, traffic congestion, safe drinking water, and efficient energy.

At least some of the associated values in the field you're exploring should match those you extracted from your list of working conditions. Take a second look at any values that don't match up. How important are they to you? What will happen if they are not satisfied on the job? Can you incorporate those personal values elsewhere? Your answers need to be brutally honest. As you continue your exploration, be sure to add to your list any additional values that occur to you.

Step 3   Calculate Your Economic Needs

Each of us grew up in an environment that provided for certain basic needs, such as food and shelter, and, to varying degrees, other needs that we now consider basic, such as cable television, e-mail, or an automobile. Needs such as privacy, space, and quiet, which at first glance may not appear to be monetary needs, may add to housing expenses and so should be considered as you examine your economic needs. For example, if you place a high value on a large, open living space for yourself, it would be difficult to satisfy that need without an associated high housing cost, especially in a densely populated city environment.

As you prepare to move into the world of work and become responsible for meeting your own basic needs, it is important to consider the salary you will need to be able to afford a satisfying standard of living. The three-step process outlined here will help you plan a budget, which in turn will allow you to evaluate the various career choices and geographic locations you are considering. The steps include (1) develop a realistic budget, (2) examine starting salaries, and (3) use a cost-of-living index.

Develop a Realistic Budget. Each of us has certain expectations for the kind of lifestyle we want to maintain. To begin the process of defining your economic needs, it will be helpful to determine what you expect to spend on routine monthly expenses. These expenses include housing, food, transportation, entertainment, utilities, loan repayments, and revolving charge accounts. You may not currently spend anything for certain items, but you probably will have to once you begin supporting yourself. As you develop this budget, be generous in your estimates, but keep in mind any items that could be reduced or eliminated. If you are not sure about the cost of a certain item, talk with family or friends who would be able to give you a realistic estimate.

If this is new or difficult for you, start to keep a log of expenses right now. You may be surprised at how much you actually spend each month for food or stamps or magazines. Household expenses and personal grooming items can often loom very large in a budget, as can auto repairs or home maintenance.

Income taxes must also be taken into consideration when examining salary requirements. State and local taxes vary, so it is difficult to calculate exactly the effect of taxes on the amount of income you need to generate. To roughly estimate the gross income necessary to generate your minimum annual salary requirement, multiply the minimum salary you have calculated by a factor of 1.35. The resulting figure will be an approximation of what your gross income would need to be, given your estimated expenses.

Examine Starting Salaries. Starting salaries for each of the career tracks are provided throughout this book. These salary figures can be used in conjunction with the cost-of-living index (discussed in the next section) to determine whether you would be able to meet your basic economic needs in a given geographic location.

Use a Cost-of-Living Index. If you are thinking about trying to get a job in a geographic region other than the one where you now live, understanding differences in the cost of living will help you come to a more informed decision about making a move. By using a cost-of-living index, you can compare salaries offered and the cost of living in different locations with what you know about the salaries offered and the cost of living in your present location.

Many variables are used to calculate the cost-of-living index. Often included are housing, groceries, utilities, transportation, health care, clothing, and entertainment expenses. Right now you do not need to worry about the details associated with calculating a given index. The main purpose of this exercise is to help you understand that pay ranges for entry-level positions may not vary greatly, but the cost of living in different locations *can* vary tremendously.

Suppose you live in Juneau, Alaska, and you are interested in working as a mechanical engineer. The U.S. Department of Labor's Bureau of Labor Statistics (bls.gov) reports that the approximate annual salary for B.S. mechanical engineers is about $50,000. Perhaps the cold weather is starting to get to you and you're considering moving to Honolulu, Hawaii, or San Diego, California. You know you can live on $50,000 in Juneau, but you want to be able to equal that salary in other locations you're considering. How much will you need to earn in those locations to do this? Figuring the cost of living for each city will show you.

In any cost-of-living index, the number 100 represents the national average cost of living, and each city is assigned an index number based on current prices in that city for the items included in the index (housing, food, salary, etc.). As you can imagine, these indices are constantly changing. In this example, Juneau's index is 100.0, Honolulu's is 198.0, and San Diego's is 169.5. In other words, it costs nearly twice as much to live in Hawaii and about one and a half times as much to live in California as it does to live in Alaska. The following table shows you how much you would have to earn in each of these cities to maintain the same style of living as you would have in Alaska on a $45,000 salary.

JOB: GEOSCIENTIST

City	Index	Equivalent Salary
Honolulu	198.0	
		$\dfrac{198.0}{100.0} \times \$50{,}000 = \$99{,}100$ in Honolulu
Juneau	100.0	
San Diego	169.5	
		$\dfrac{169.5}{100.0} \times \$50{,}000 = \$84{,}750$ in San Diego
Juneau	100.0	

This means that you'll need to make significantly more in both warmer cities to maintain your current standard of living. On the other hand, just think of the money you'll save on not having to pay heating costs and for winter clothes!

If you have an aversion to math, there are a variety of salary converters online that will do the work for you. Simply type "salary conversion" or "salary calculator" into a search engine and you'll find plenty of free choices.

You can work through a similar exercise for any type of job you are considering and for many locations when current salary information is available. It will be worth your time to undertake this analysis if you are seriously considering a relocation. By doing so you will be able to make an informed choice.

Step 4 Explore Your Longer-Term Goals

There is no question that when we first begin working, our goals are to use our skills and education in a job that will reward us with employment, income, and status relative to the preparation we brought with us to this position. If we are not being paid as much as we feel we should for our level of education or if job demands don't provide the intellectual stimulation we had hoped for, we experience unhappiness and as a result often seek other employment.

Most jobs we consider "good" are those that fulfill our basic "lower-level" needs of security, food, clothing, shelter, income, and productive work. But even when our basic needs are met and our jobs are secure and productive, we as individuals are constantly changing. As we change, the demands and expectations we place on our jobs may change. Fortunately, some jobs grow and change with us, and this explains why some people are happy throughout many years in a job.

But more often people are bigger than the jobs they fill. We have more goals and needs than any job could satisfy. These are "higher-level" needs of self-esteem, companionship, affection, and an increasing desire to feel we are employing ourselves in the most effective way possible. Not all of these higher-level needs can be met through employment, but for as long as we are employed, we increasingly demand that our jobs play their part in moving us along the path to fulfillment.

Another obvious but important fact is that we change as we mature. Although our jobs also have the potential for change, they may not change as frequently or as markedly as we do. There are increasingly fewer one-job, one-employer careers; we must think about a work future that may involve voluntary or forced moves from employer to employer. Because of that very real possibility, we need to take advantage of the opportunities in each position we hold. Acquiring the skills and competencies associated with each position will keep us viable and attractive as employees. This is particularly true in a job market that not only is technology/computer dependent, but also is populated with more and more small, self-transforming organizations rather than the large, seemingly stable organizations of the past.

If you are considering a position as a petroleum engineer with a major oil company, you would gain a better perspective on this career if you talked to a recent graduate who is now working full-time at the company; a mid-level engineer, who has been with the company five to eight years; and a senior manager or director, who has been with the company or in the industry for more than ten years. Ask these people to grant you an informational interview, and come prepared with questions about their experiences with the company and in the industry, advice they have for new engineers, and how they obtained their current positions.

Step 5   Enumerate Your Skill Base

In terms of the job search, skills can be thought of as capabilities that can be developed in school, at work, or by volunteering and then used in specific job settings. Many studies have documented the kinds of skills that employers seek in entry-level applicants. For example, some of the most desired skills for individuals interested in the teaching profession are the ability to interact effectively with students one-on-one, to manage a classroom, to adapt to varying situations as necessary, and to get involved in school activities. Business employers have also identified important qualities, including enthusiasm for the employer's product or service, a businesslike mind, the ability to follow written or oral instructions, the ability to demonstrate self-control, the confidence to suggest new ideas, the ability to communicate with all members of a group, an awareness of cultural differences, and loyalty, to name just a few. You will find that many of these skills are also in the repertoire of qualities demanded in your college major.

To be successful in obtaining any given job, you must be able to demonstrate that you possess a certain mix of skills that will allow you to carry out the duties required by that job. This skill mix will vary a great deal from job to job; to determine the skills necessary for the jobs you are seeking, you can read job advertisements or more generic job descriptions, such as those found later in this book. If you want to be effective in the job search, you must directly show employers that you possess the skills needed to be successful in filling the position. These skills will initially be described on your résumé and then discussed again during the interview process.

Skills are either general or specific. To develop a list of skills relevant to employers, you must first identify the general skills you possess, then list specific skills you have to offer, and, finally, examine which of these skills employers are seeking.

Identify Your General Skills. Because you possess or will possess a college degree, employers will assume that you can read and write, perform certain basic computations, think critically, and communicate effectively. Employers will want to see that you have acquired these skills, and they will want to know which additional general skills you possess.

One way to begin identifying skills is to write an experiential diary. An experiential diary lists all the tasks you were responsible for completing for each job you've held and then outlines the skills required to do those tasks. You may list several skills for any given task. This diary allows you to distinguish between the tasks you performed and the underlying skills required to complete those tasks. Here's an example:

Tasks	Skills
Circuit design	Use of basic test equipment (voltmeter, oscilloscope, etc.) to take test data and troubleshoot problems
Programming industrial controls	PLC experience
Presentations to engineering teams	Organization of thoughts and clear communication skills

For each job or experience you have participated in, develop a worksheet based on the example shown here. On a résumé, you may want to describe these skills rather than simply listing tasks. Skills are easier for the employer to appreciate, especially when your experience is very different from the employment you are seeking. In addition to helping you identify general skills, this experiential diary will prepare you to speak more effectively in an interview about the qualifications you possess.

Identify Your Specific Skills. It may be easier to identify your specific skills because you can definitely say whether you can speak other languages, program a computer, draft a map or diagram, or edit a document using appropriate symbols and terminology.

Using your experiential diary, identify the points in your history where you learned how to do something very specific, and decide whether you have a beginning, intermediate, or advanced knowledge of how to use that particular skill. Right now, be sure to list *every* specific skill you have, and don't consider whether you like using the skill. Write down a list of specific skills you have acquired and the level of competence you possess—beginning, intermediate, or advanced.

Relate Your Skills to Employers. You probably have thought about a couple of different jobs you might be interested in obtaining, and one way to begin relating the general and specific skills you possess to a potential employer's needs is to read actual advertisements for these types of positions (see Part Two for resources listing actual job openings).

Let's say that your engineering internship or co-op job has been in the manufacturing sector and you have worked on lean production projects, statistical process control, and simulation modeling. When you apply to other manufacturing companies, your tasks and the skills that you used will be widely understood. But what if you are also interested in exploring consulting career opportunities? How do you relate your manufacturing skills to the needs of a consulting firm?

The first step is to spend some time exploring the websites of the consulting firms that you are interested in. What types of projects do they feature? Where do they work? Who are some of their clients? What values do they talk about? If their websites list positions available, what are the skills and qualities that they seek in job candidates? Make a list for each company. When you begin to construct your résumé and prepare for interviews, this information will help you focus your communication on the things that are most important to this type of employer.

JOB: CONSULTING ENGINEER

General	Specific
Infrastructure Solutions	Data centers, networking, predictive operations, end-user computing, and security
Radio Frequency Identification (RFID)	Wireless technology, tagging/ tracking technologies
Logistics	Statistics, simulation, business analytics
Supply Chain	Distribution optimization, sales, sourcing, and procurement
Business Research	Data mining, interviewing techniques, information synthesis, project management
Enterprise Resource Planning	SAP, Oracle, process integration

The second step is to think about *how* you did your intern or co-op job, not just *what* you did. For example, did you collect data that you and/or others analyzed? Did you have to give regular reports to your team and/or supervisor on the work that you were doing? Were there regular meetings where your team had to make presentations to senior management? Did you interact with suppliers to make sure that they understood the requirements of the manufacturer? Did you make presentations to your team, to management, or to outside groups? Did you learn and use software applications not available to you on-campus? Did you make recommendations that were implemented by your team, unit, division, or company? These are the types of skills that a consulting firm will want to know that you possess.

There is not a job description, in any field, that doesn't stress the need for good communication skills. Saying that you have them, does not make it so. Therefore, make a list of examples of your communication style from both classroom and work situations. You might consider developing a portfolio of your best writing samples, including technical papers, PowerPoint presentations, business correspondence, and so on. If you or your school have confidentiality agreements with any people or organizations, make sure you have their written permission to use any writing sample that is based on your work with them. In addition, if any of your writing samples are team efforts, be sure to give credit to other members of your team. If you didn't play a significant role in writing a team paper, it is best not to use it in a portfolio because it is not an example of *your* best work.

EXAMPLES OF YOUR COMMUNICATION SKILLS
Weekly reports to teams at your intern or co-op job
PowerPoint presentations on classroom or work projects
Instructions written for school project teams
Letters written to secure funding or supplies for a school
     project or activity
Minutes from student organization meetings
Final reports in capstone courses

Step 6   Recognize Your Preferred Skills

In the previous section you developed a comprehensive list of skills that relate to particular career paths that are of interest to you. You can now relate these to skills that you prefer to use. We all use a wide range of skills (some researchers say individuals have a repertoire of about five hundred skills), but we may not particularly be interested in using all of them in our work. There may be some skills that come to us more naturally or that we use successfully time and time again and that we want to continue to use; these are best described as our preferred skills. For this exercise use the list of skills that you created for the previous section, and decide which of them you are *most interested in using* in future work and how often you would like to use them. You might be interested in using some skills only occasionally, while others you would like to use more regularly. You probably also have skills that you hope you can use constantly.

As you examine job announcements, look for matches between this list of preferred skills and the qualifications described in the advertisements. These skills should be highlighted on your résumé and discussed in job interviews.

Step 7   Assess Skills Needing Further Development

Previously you compiled a list of general and specific skills required for given positions. You already possess some of these skills; those that remain to be developed are your underdeveloped skills.

If you are just beginning the job search, there may be gaps between the qualifications required for some of the jobs you're considering and the skills you possess. The thought of having to admit to and talk about these underdeveloped skills, especially in a job interview, is a frightening one. One way to put a healthy perspective on this subject is to target and relate your exploration of underdeveloped skills to the types of positions you are seeking. Recognizing these shortcomings and planning to overcome them with either on-the-job training or additional formal education can be a positive way to address the concept of underdeveloped skills.

On your worksheet or in your journal, make a list of up to five general or specific skills required for the positions you're interested in that you *don't currently possess*. For each item list an idea you have for specific action you could take to acquire that skill. Do some brainstorming to come up with possible actions. If you have a hard time generating ideas, talk to people currently working in this type of position, professionals in your college career services office, trusted friends, family members, or members of related professional associations.

In the chapter on interviewing, we will discuss in detail how to effectively address questions about underdeveloped skills. Generally speaking, though, employers want genuine answers to these types of questions. They want you to reveal "the real you," and they also want to see how you answer difficult questions. In taking the positive, targeted approach discussed previously, you show the employer that you are willing to continue to learn and that you have a plan for strengthening your job qualifications.

Use Your Self-Assessment

Exploring entry-level career options can be an exciting experience if you have good resources available and will take the time to use them. Can you effectively complete the following tasks?

1. Understand your personality traits and relate them to career choices
2. Define your personal values
3. Determine your economic needs

4. Explore longer-term goals
5. Understand your skill base
6. Recognize your preferred skills
7. Express a willingness to improve on your underdeveloped skills

If so, then you can more meaningfully participate in the job search process by writing a more effective résumé, finding job titles that represent work you are interested in doing, locating job sites that will provide the opportunity for you to use your strengths and skills, networking in an informed way, participating in focused interviews, getting the most out of follow-up contacts, and evaluating job offers to find those that create a good match between you and the employer. The remaining chapters in Part One guide you through these next steps in the job search process. For many job seekers, this process can take anywhere from three months to a year to implement. The time you will need to put into your job search will depend on the type of job you want and the geographic location where you'd like to work. Think of your effort as a job in itself, requiring you to set aside time each week to complete the needed work. Carefully undertaken efforts may reduce the time you need for your job search.

2

The Résumé and Cover Letter

The task of writing a résumé may seem overwhelming if you are unfamiliar with this type of document, but there are some easily understood techniques that can and should be used. This section was written to help you understand the purpose of the résumé, the different types of formats available, and how to write the sections that contain information traditionally found on a résumé. We will present examples and explanations that address questions frequently posed by people writing their first résumé or updating an old one.

Even within the formats and suggestions given, however, there are infinite variations. True, most follow one of the outlines suggested, but you should feel free to adjust the résumé to suit your needs and make it expressive of your life and experience.

Why Write a Résumé?

The purpose of a résumé is to convince an employer that you should be interviewed. Whether you're mailing, faxing, or e-mailing this document, you'll want to present enough information to show that you can make an immediate and valuable contribution to an organization. A résumé is not an indepth historical or legal document; later in the job search process you may be asked to document your entire work history on an application form and attest to its validity. The résumé should, instead, highlight relevant information pertaining directly to the organization that will receive the document or to the type of position you are seeking.

We will discuss the chronological and digital résumés in detail here. Functional and targeted résumés, which are used much less often, are briefly discussed. The reasons for using one type of résumé over another and the typical format for each are addressed in the following sections.

The Chronological Résumé

The chronological résumé is the most common of the various résumé formats and therefore the format that employers are most used to receiving. This type of résumé is easy to read and understand because it details the chronological progression of jobs you have held. (See Exhibit 2.1.) It begins with your most recent employment and works back in time. If you have a solid work history or have experience that provided growth and development in your duties and responsibilities, a chronological résumé will highlight these achievements. The typical elements of a chronological résumé include the heading, a career objective, educational background, employment experience, activities, and references.

The Heading

The heading consists of your name, address, telephone number, and other means of contact. This may include a fax number, e-mail address, and your home-page address. If you are using a shared e-mail account or a parent's business fax, be sure to let others who use these systems know that you may receive important professional correspondence via these systems. You wouldn't want to miss a vital e-mail or fax! Likewise, if your résumé directs readers to a personal home page on the Web, be certain it's a professional personal home page designed to be viewed and appreciated by a prospective employer. This may mean making substantial changes in the home page you currently mount on the Web.

The Objective

Without a doubt the objective statement is the most challenging part of the résumé for most writers. Even for individuals who have decided on a career path, it can be difficult to encapsulate all they want to say in one or two brief sentences. For job seekers who are unfocused or unclear about their intentions, trying to write this section can inhibit the entire résumé writing process.

Keep the objective as short as possible and no longer than two short sentences.

Exhibit 2.1
CHRONOLOGICAL RÉSUMÉ

JOHN J. DOE

Campus Address	Permanent Address
224 University Place	506 Apollo Street
Downstate, IL 60000	Mundelein, IL 69999
Phone: 555-555-1234	Phone: 555-777-6789
Cell: 555-123-4567	Fax: 555-987-6543
Website: www.mmuv.edu/j-doe	
E-mail: j-doe@mmuv.edu	

OBJECTIVE

Seeking an entry-level position in an automated manufacturing organization where I can use knowledge gained about lean manufacturing, statistical process control, and simulation through my co-op experience.

EDUCATION

B.S. Mechanical Engineering, 2007
Concentration: Manufacturing
Midwestern University

HONORS

Name on patent #1,234,567, new fastener product for Smith & Jones
   Manufacturing, Inc.
Tau Beta Pi, Engineering Honor Society
Kappa Theta Epsilon, Cooperative Education Honor Society
Who's Who in Colleges and Universities

SKILLS

Kaizen training; AutoMod, ProEngineer, MATLAB, FEA Software, Dreamweaver, MS Access and Excel; Database programming language O++, C++, Visual Basic, Java, JavaScript, HTML, SQL; Fluent in Spanish, Study Abroad in Madrid, Spain, 2006

continued

WORK EXPERIENCE

Manufacturing Engineering Co-op Smith & Jones Manufacturing, Inc., Mundelein, IL, 2003–2006. Completed assignments in various departments as a part of an overall training program:

New Product Development—participated in two Kaizen events; provided design and drafting support for new fastener product line using ProEngineer software; built, stress tested, evaluated, and shipped prototypes to customers. Project has the potential to expand market share by up to 15 percent.

Manufacturing Engineering—designed secondary tooling for new fastener assembly equipment, prepared report on recommended changes to supply-chain management. Recommendations implemented companywide.

Quality Control—provided in-process manufacturing inspection for the plant manager.

Shipping—developed database for plant material inventory; scheduled vendors' warehouse pickup.

Purchasing—provided raw material purchasing support to learn entire product line.

Teaching Assistant, Department of Biology, Midwestern University, 2002–Present. Set up experiments; designed lesson plans; delivered lectures in a biology lab for 13 students ages 6–8 participating in a gifted and talented program. Received Undergraduate Teaching Assistant Award from Department of Biology.

Lifeguard, Ace Property Owner's Association, Mundelein, IL, Summers 2001–2002.

ACTIVITIES

Student Government, Vice President, 2006–2007

American Society of Mechanical Engineering, Student Chapter, President, 2005–2006

Delta Upsilon Social Fraternity, President, 2005–2006

New Student Orientation Leader, School of Engineering, 2003

Residence Hall, Committee Chair, 2005

Varsity Hockey Team, Second Place, Midwest Sports Conference, 2006

Katrina Disaster Relief Volunteer, 2006

Choose one of the following types of objective statement:

1. General Objective Statement

- An entry-level educational programming coordinator position

2. Position-Focused Objective

- To obtain the position of conference coordinator at State College

3. Industry-Focused Objective

- To begin a career as a sales representative in the cruise line industry

4. Summary of Qualifications Statement

A bachelor's degree in chemical engineering and four semesters of progressively responsible co-op experience in the chemical industry, which involved testing and developing technical specifications for a new analyzer system and supporting Technical Service in the area of organic and inorganic pigments, pigment dispersions, additives, and universal colorants for specialized coatings.

Support Your Objective. A résumé that contains any one of these types of objective statements should then go on to demonstrate why you are qualified to get the position. Listing academic degrees can be one way to indicate qualifications. Another demonstration would be in the way previous experiences, both volunteer and paid, are described. Without this kind of documentation in the body of the résumé, the objective looks unsupported. Think of the résumé as telling a connected story about you. All the elements should work together to form a coherent picture that ideally should relate to your statement of objective.

Education

This section of your résumé should indicate the exact name of the degree you will receive or have received, spelled out completely with no abbreviations. The degree is generally listed after the objective, followed by the institution name and location, and then the month and year of graduation. This section could also include your academic minor, grade point average (GPA), and appearance on the Dean's List or President's List.

If you have enough space, you might want to include a section listing courses related to the field in which you are seeking work. The best use of a "related courses" section would be to list some course work that is not traditionally associated with the major. Perhaps you took several computer courses outside your degree that will be helpful and related to the job prospects you are entertaining. Several education section examples are shown here:

- Master of Engineering Management, Duke University, Durham, NC, May 2007; Emphasis: Innovative Management
- Bachelor of Science, Industrial Engineering, Georgia Tech University, Atlanta, GA, August 2007; Concentration: Large-scale optimization and computing; Minor: Economics; GPA 3.75/4.0
- Master of Science, Electrical Engineering, Case Western Reserve University, Cleveland, OH, May 2007; Thesis: VLSI Design for Image Processors

Experience

The experience section of your résumé should be the most substantial part and should take up most of the space on the page. Employers want to see what kind of work history you have. They will look at your range of experiences, longevity in jobs, and specific tasks you are able to complete. This section may also be called "work experience," "related experience," "employment history," or "employment." No matter what you call this section, some important points to remember are the following:

1. **Describe your duties** as they relate to the position you are seeking.
2. **Emphasize major responsibilities** and indicate increases in responsibility. Include all relevant employment experiences: summer, part-time, internships, cooperative education, or self-employment.
3. **Emphasize skills**, especially those that transfer from one situation to another. The fact that you coordinated a student organization,

chaired meetings, supervised others, and managed a budget leads one to suspect that you could coordinate other things as well.

4. **Use descriptive job titles** that provide information about what you did. A "Student Intern" should be more specifically stated as, for example, "Magazine Operations Intern." "Volunteer" is also too general; a title such as "Peer Writing Tutor" would be more appropriate.

5. **Create word pictures** by using active verbs to start sentences. Describe *results* you have produced in the work you have done.

A limp description would say something such as the following: "My duties included helping with production, proofreading, and editing. I used a design and page layout program." An action statement would be stated as follows: "Coordinated and assisted in the creative marketing of brochures and seminar promotions, becoming proficient in Quark."

Remember, an accomplishment is simply a result, a final measurable product that people can relate to. A duty is not a result; it is an obligation— every job holder has duties. For an effective résumé, list as many results as you can. To make the most of the limited space you have and to give your description impact, carefully select appropriate and accurate descriptors.

Here are some traits that employers tell us they like to see:

- Teamwork
- Energy and motivation
- Learning and using new skills
- Versatility
- Critical thinking
- Understanding how profits are created
- Organizational acumen
- Risk taking
- Communicating directly and clearly, in both writing and speaking
- Willingness to admit mistakes
- High personal standards

Solutions to Frequently Encountered Problems

Repetitive Employment with the Same Employer

EMPLOYMENT: The Foot Locker, Portland, Oregon. Summer 2001, 2002, 2003. Initially employed in high school as salesclerk. Because of successful performance, asked to return next two summers at higher pay with added responsibility. Ranked as the #2 salesperson the first summer and #1 the next two summers. Assisted in arranging eye-catching retail displays; served as manager of other summer workers during owner's absence.

A Large Number of Jobs
EMPLOYMENT: Recent Hospitality Industry Experience: Affiliated with four upscale hotel/restaurant complexes (September 2001–February 2004), where I worked part- and full-time as a waiter, bartender, disc jockey, and bookkeeper to produce income for college.

Several Positions with the Same Employer
EMPLOYMENT: Coca-Cola Bottling Co., Burlington, Vermont, 2001–2004. In four years, I received three promotions, each with increased pay and responsibility.

Summer Sales Coordinator: Promoted to hire, train, and direct efforts of add-on staff of fifteen college-age route salespeople hired to meet summer peak demand for product.

Sales Administrator: Promoted to run home office sales desk, managing accounts and associated delivery schedules for professional sales force of ten people. Intensive phone work, daily interaction with all personnel, and strong knowledge of product line required.

Route Salesperson: Summer employment to travel and tourism industry sites that use Coke products. Met specific schedule demands, used good communication skills with wide variety of customers, and demonstrated strong selling skills. Named salesperson of the month for July and August of that year.

Questions Résumé Writers Often Ask

How Far Back Should I Go in Terms of Listing Past Jobs?
Usually, listing three or four jobs should suffice. If you did something back in high school that has a bearing on your future aspirations for employment, by all means list the job. As you progress through your college career, high school jobs will be replaced on the résumé by college employment.

Should I Differentiate Between Paid and Nonpaid Employment?

Most employers are not initially concerned about how much you were paid. They are eager to know how much responsibility you held in your past employment. There is no need to specify that your work was as a volunteer if you had significant responsibilities.

How Should I Represent My Accomplishments or Work-Related Responsibilities?

Succinctly, but fully. In other words, give the employer enough information to arouse curiosity but not so much detail that you leave nothing to the imagination. Besides, some jobs merit more lengthy explanations than others. Be sure to convey any information that can give an employer a better understanding of the depth of your involvement at work. Did you supervise others? How many? Did your efforts result in a more efficient operation? How much did you increase efficiency? Did you handle a budget? How much? Were you promoted in a short time? Did you work two jobs at once or fifteen hours per week after high school? Where appropriate, quantify.

Should the Work Section Always Follow the Education Section on the Résumé?

Always lead with your strengths. If your education closely relates to the employment you now seek, put this section after the objective. If your education does not closely relate but you have a surplus of good work experiences, consider reversing the order of your sections to lead with employment, followed by education.

How Should I Present My Activities, Honors, Awards, Professional Societies, and Affiliations?

This section of the résumé can add valuable information for an employer to consider if used correctly. The rule of thumb for information in this section is to include only those activities that are in some way relevant to the objective stated on your résumé. If you can draw a valid connection between your activities and your objective, include them; if not, leave them out.

Professional affiliations and honors should all be listed; especially important are those related to your job objective. Social clubs and activities need not be a part of your résumé unless you hold a significant office or you are looking for a position related to your membership. Be aware that most prospective employers' principal concerns are related to your employability, not your social life. If you have any, publications can be included as an addendum to your résumé.

How Should I Handle References?

The use of references is considered a part of the interview process, and they should never be listed on a résumé. You would always provide references to a potential employer if requested to, so it is not even necessary to include this section on the résumé if space does not permit. If space is available, it is acceptable to include the following statement:

- References furnished upon request.

The Functional Résumé

A functional résumé departs from a chronological résumé in that it organizes information by specific accomplishments in various settings: previous jobs, volunteer work, associations, and so forth. This type of résumé permits you to stress the substance of your experiences rather than the position titles you have held. You should consider using a functional résumé if you have held a series of similar jobs that relied on the same skills or abilities. There are many good books in which you can find examples of functional résumés, including *How to Write a Winning Resume* or *Resumes Made Easy*.

The Targeted Résumé

The targeted résumé focuses on specific work-related capabilities you can bring to a given position within an organization. Past achievements are listed to highlight your capabilities and the work history section is abbreviated.

Digital Résumés

Today's employers have to manage an enormous number of résumés. One of the most frequent complaints the writers of this series hear from students is the failure of employers to even acknowledge the receipt of a résumé and cover letter. Frequently, the reason for this poor response or nonresponse is the volume of applications received for every job. In an attempt to better manage the considerable labor investment involved in processing large numbers of résumés, many employers are requiring digital submission of résumés. There are two types of digital résumés: those that can be e-mailed or posted to a website, called *electronic résumés,* and those that can be "read" by a computer, commonly called *scannable résumés.* Though the format may be a bit different from the traditional "paper" résumé, the goal of both types of digital résumés is the same—to get you an interview! These résumés must be designed to be "technologically friendly." What that basically means to you is that they should be free of graphics and fancy formatting. (See Exhibit 2.2.)

Electronic Résumés

Sometimes referred to as plain-text résumés, electronic résumés are designed to be e-mailed to an employer or posted to one of many commercial Internet databases such as Careerbuilder.com, America's Job Bank (ajb.dni.us), or Monster.com.

Some technical considerations:

- Electronic résumés must be written in American Standard Code for Information Interchange (ASCII), which is simply a plain-text format. These characters are universally recognized so that every computer can accurately read and understand them. To create an ASCII file of your current résumé, open your document, then save it as a text or ASCII file. This will eliminate all formatting. Edit as needed using your computer's text editor application.
- Use a standard-width typeface. Courier is a good choice because it is the font associated with ASCII in most systems.
- Use a font size of 11 to 14 points. A 12-point font is considered standard.
- Your margin should be left-justified.
- Do not exceed sixty-five characters per line because the word-wrap function doesn't operate in ASCII.
- Do not use boldface, italics, underlining, bullets, or various font sizes. Instead, use asterisks, plus signs, or all capital letters when you want to emphasize something.
- Avoid graphics and shading.
- Use as many "keywords" as you possibly can. These are words or phrases usually relating to skills or experience that either are specifically used in the job announcement or are popular buzzwords in the industry.
- Minimize abbreviations.

Exhibit 2.2
DIGITAL RÉSUMÉ

JOHN J. DOE
224 University Place
Downstate, IL 60000
Phone: 555-555-1234
Cell: 555-123-4567
Website: www.mmuv.edu/j-doe
E-mail: j-doe@mmuv.edu

Put your name at the
top on its own line.

Put your phone number
on its own line.

KEYWORD SUMMARY
*Mechanical Engineering
*Manufacturing Engineering
*Lean
*Simulation
*Statistical Process Control (SPC)

Keywords make your
résumé easier to find in
a database.

EDUCATION
B.S. Mechanical Engineering, 2007
Concentration: Manufacturing
Overall GPA 3.6/4.0; GPA in major 3.9/4.0
Midwestern University, Downstate, IL

Use a standard-width
typeface.

RELEVANT COURSES
*Advanced Manufacturing Technology
*Mechanics of Machinery
*Relation of Materials to Design
*Econometrics
*Engineering Optimization

Use a space between
asterisk and text.

EXPERIENCE
Manufacturing Engineering Co-op, 2003-2006.
Smith & Jones Manufacturing, Inc., Mundelein, IL.
*Completed assignments in various departments as a
    part of an overall training program:
*New Product Development—participated in two
    Kaizen events; provided design and drafting

Capitalize letters to
emphasize heading

continued

support for new fastener product line using
ProEngineer software; built, stress tested,
evaluated, and shipped prototypes to customers.
Project has the potential to expand market share
by up to 15 percent.

*Manufacturing Engineering—designed secondary
tooling for new fastener assembly equipment,
prepared report on recommended changes to
supply chain management. Recommendations
implemented companywide.

*Quality Control—provided in-process manufacturing
inspection for the plant manager.

*Shipping—developed database for plant material
inventory; scheduled vendors' warehouse pickup.

*Purchasing—provided raw material purchasing
support to learn entire product line.

No line should exceed sixty-five characters.

End each line by hitting the ENTER (or RETURN) key.

- Your name should be the first line of text.
- Conduct a "test run" by e-mailing your résumé to yourself and a friend before you send it to the employer. See how it transmits, and make any changes you need to. Continue to test it until it's exactly how you want it to look.
- Unless an employer specifically requests that you send the résumé in the form of an attachment, don't. Employers can encounter problems opening a document as an attachment, and there are always viruses to consider.
- Don't forget your cover letter. Send it along with your résumé as a single message.

Scannable Résumés

Some companies are relying on technology to narrow the candidate pool for available job openings. Electronic Applicant Tracking uses imaging to scan, sort, and store résumé elements in a database. Then, through OCR (Optical Character Recognition) software, the computer scans the résumés for keywords and phrases. To have the best chance at getting an interview, you want to increase the number of "hits"—matches of your skills, abilities, experience, and education to those the computer is scanning for—your résumé will get. You can see how critical using the right keywords is for this type of résumé.

Technical considerations include:

- Again, do not use boldface (newer systems may be able to read this, but many older ones won't), italics, underlining, bullets, shading, graphics, or multiple font sizes. Instead, for emphasis, use asterisks, plus signs, or all capital letters. Minimize abbreviations.
- Use a popular typeface such as Courier, Helvetica, Arial, or Palatino. Avoid decorative fonts.
- Font size should be between 11 and 14 points.
- Do not compress the spacing between letters.
- Use horizontal and vertical lines sparingly; the computer may misread them as the letters *L* or *I*.
- Left-justify the text.
- Do not use parentheses or brackets around telephone numbers, and be sure your phone number is on its own line of text.
- Your name should be the first line of text and on its own line. If your résumé is longer than one page, be sure to put your name on the top of all pages.
- Use a traditional résumé structure. The chronological format may work best.
- Use nouns that are skill-focused, such as *management, writer,* and *programming.* This is different from traditional paper résumés, which use action-oriented verbs.
- Laser printers produce the finest copies. Avoid dot-matrix printers.
- Use standard, light-colored paper with text on one side only. Since the higher the contrast, the better, your best choice is black ink on white paper.
- Always send original copies. If you must fax, set the fax on fine mode, not standard.
- Do not staple or fold your résumé. This can confuse the computer.
- Before you send your scannable résumé, be certain the employer uses this technology. If you can't determine this, you may want to send two versions (scannable and traditional) to be sure your résumé gets considered.

Résumé Production and Other Tips

An ink-jet printer is the preferred option for printing your résumé. Begin by printing just a few copies. You may find a small error or you may simply want to make some changes, and it is less frustrating and less expensive if you print in small batches.

Résumé paper color should be carefully chosen. You should consider the types of employers who will receive your résumé and the types of positions for which you are applying. Use white or ivory paper for traditional or conservative employers or for higher-level positions.

Black ink on sharp, white paper can be harsh on the reader's eyes. Think about an ivory or cream paper that will provide less contrast and be easier to read. Pink, green, and blue tints should generally be avoided.

Many résumé writers buy packages of matching envelopes and cover sheet stationery that, although not absolutely necessary, help convey a professional impression.

If you'll be producing many cover letters at home, be sure you have high-quality printing equipment. Learn standard envelope formats for business, and retain a copy of every cover letter you send out. You can use the copies to take notes of any telephone conversations that may occur.

If attending a job fair, either carry a briefcase or place your résumé in a nicely covered legal-size pad holder.

The Cover Letter

The cover letter provides you with the opportunity to tailor your résumé by telling the prospective employer how you can be a benefit to the organization. It allows you to highlight aspects of your background that are not already discussed in your résumé and that might be especially relevant to the organization you are contacting or to the position you are seeking. Every résumé should have a cover letter enclosed when you send it out. Unlike the résumé, which may be mass-produced, a cover letter is most effective when it is individually prepared and focused on the particular requirements of the organization in question.

A good cover letter should supplement the résumé and motivate the reader to review the résumé. The format shown in Exhibit 2.3 (see page 35) is only a suggestion to help you decide what information to include in a cover letter.

Begin the cover letter with your street address six lines down from the top. Leave three to five lines between the date and the name of the person to whom you are addressing the cover letter. Make sure you leave one blank line between the salutation and the body of the letter and between paragraphs. After typing "Sincerely," leave four blank lines and type your name. This should leave plenty of room for your signature. A sample cover letter is shown in Exhibit 2.4 on page 36.

The following guidelines will help you write good cover letters:

1. Be sure to type your letter neatly; ensure there are no misspellings.
2. Avoid unusual typefaces, such as script.
3. Address the letter to an individual, using the person's name and title. To obtain this information, call the company. If answering a blind newspaper advertisement, address the letter "To Whom It May Concern" or omit the salutation.
4. Be sure your cover letter directly indicates the position you are applying for and tells why you are qualified to fill it.
5. Send the original letter, not a photocopy, with your résumé. Keep a copy for your records.
6. Make your cover letter no more than one page.
7. Include a phone number where you can be reached.
8. Avoid trite language and have someone read the letter over to react to its tone, content, and mechanics.
9. For your own information, record the date you send out each letter and résumé.

Exhibit 2.3
COVER LETTER FORMAT

Your Street Address
Your Town, State, Zip
Phone Number
Fax Number
E-mail

Date

Name
Title
Organization
Address

Dear _____:

First Paragraph. In this paragraph state the reason for the letter, name the specific position or type of work you are applying for, and indicate from which resource (career services office, website, newspaper, contact, employment service) you learned of this opening. The first paragraph can also be used to inquire about future openings.

Second Paragraph. Indicate why you are interested in this position, the company, or its products or services and what you can do for the employer. If you are a recent graduate, explain how your academic background makes you a qualified candidate. Try not to repeat the same information found in the résumé.

Third Paragraph. Refer the reader to the enclosed résumé for more detailed information.

Fourth Paragraph. In this paragraph say what you will do to follow up on your letter. For example, state that you will call by a certain date to set up an interview or to find out if the company will be recruiting in your area. Finish by indicating your willingness to answer any questions the recipient may have. Be sure you have provided your phone number.

Sincerely,

Type your name

Enclosure

Exhibit 2.4
SAMPLE COVER LETTER

224 University Place
Downstate, IL 60000
Phone: 555-555-1234
Cell: 555-123-4567
October 15, 2001
E-mail: j-doe@mmuv.edu

Mr. Michael T. Smith
Chief Design Engineer
Race Car Designs, Ltd.
98765 Speedway Junction
Raceland, AZ 99999

Dear Mr. Smith:

In May of 2008, I will graduate from Midwestern University with a bachelor of science degree in aerospace engineering. I read of your entry-level design position in the January issue of *Racing Monthly*. I am interested in the possibilities it offers.

The ad indicated that you were looking for someone with basic design experience and good communication skills. I believe that I possess those qualities. My academic preparation includes course work in aerodynamics and structures, advanced finite element analysis, and machine design and fabrication. In addition, my hands-on experience includes participation in both the suspension and aerodynamic groups of my university's SAE Race Car Team, a short-term assignment with the World Sports Car Team, and a variety of experiences at a NASA facility during my Co-op work periods. These projects included the investigation of vibrational characteristics and the determination of equations for wind velocity for a navigation system and for a finite element model for a flexible space structure.

A résumé is enclosed for your review. I would appreciate meeting with you to discuss how my education and experience would meet your needs. I will contact your office next week to discuss an interview. I appreciate your time.

Sincerely,

John J. Doe

Enclosures

3

Researching Careers and Networking

What do they call the job you want? One reason for confusion is perhaps a mistaken assumption that a college education provides job training. In most cases it does not. Of course, applied fields such as engineering, management, or education provide specific skills for the workplace as well as an education. Regardless, your overall college education exposes you to numerous fields of study and teaches you quantitative reasoning, critical thinking, writing, and speaking, all of which can be successfully applied to a number of different job fields. But it still remains up to you to choose a job field and to learn how to articulate the benefits of your education in a way the employer will appreciate.

"What can I really do with my degree?" Biomedical engineering majors are much more likely to pose this question than students earning mechanical, electrical, or chemical engineering degrees because it is not clear how to begin their careers with a B.S. degree. Your friend who's an electrical engineering major knows she'll most likely start her career with a manufacturing firm. Or your friend who's a chemical engineering major is planning to go into specialty chemicals. If you are not sure what kind of work you are qualified for, or the type of employer that would hire you, this chapter will help you gain that understanding.

Collect Job Titles

The world of employment is a complex place, so you need to become a bit of an explorer and adventurer and be willing to try a variety of techniques to develop a list of possible occupations that might use your talents and education. You might find computerized interest inventories, reference books and other sources, and classified ads helpful in this respect. Once you have a list of possibilities that you are interested in and qualified for, you can move on to find out what kinds of organizations have these job titles.

Computerized Interest Inventories

One way to begin collecting job titles is to identify a number of jobs that call for your degree and the particular skills and interests you identified as part of the self-assessment process. There are excellent interactive career-guidance programs on the market to help you produce such selected lists of possible job titles. Most of these are available at colleges and at some larger town and city libraries. Two of the industry leaders are *CHOICES* and *DISCOVER*. Both allow you to enter interests, values, educational background, and other information to produce lists of possible occupations and industries. Each of the resources listed here will produce different job title lists. Some job titles will appear again and again, while others will be unique to a particular source. Investigate all of them!

Reference Sources

Books on the market that may be available through your local library or career counseling office also suggest various occupations related to specific majors. The following are only a few of the many good books on the market: *The College Board Guide to 150 College Majors* and *College Majors and Careers: A Resource Guide for Effective Life Planning* both by Paul Phifer, and *Kaplan's What to Study: 101 Fields in a Flash*. All of these books list possible job titles within the academic major.

Not every engineering employer offers the same type of work setting. In fact, engineering offers a wide range of work environments, no matter which engineering field you have pursued. For example, mechanical engineers can work in high-pressure manufacturing facilities or clean-room environments, where they interact with only a few people. Industrial engineers can work in logistics departments, which collect data, and can interact with a wide variety of vendors and clients. Civil and environmental engineers can work for private construction firms or public agencies such as the EPA or transportation departments. Aerospace engineers can work for aerospace companies such as Boeing or government agencies such as NASA. Some even work for racing teams. Obviously, this wide range of employers offers different "cultures" and expectations for the people they employ.

If you majored in chemical engineering, with a concentration in reaction engineering, you might enjoy working with automated laboratory reactors that use online data acquisition and analysis. However, if you enjoy moving from place to place and meeting new people, you could apply the same skills with an industry consulting firm.

As an engineer, you don't have to give up your well-developed skills to find work that you will enjoy doing. Engineering work can be found in a number of different and interesting settings to match your personality and values.

Each job title deserves your consideration. Like removing the layers of an onion, the search for job titles can go on and on! As you spend time doing this activity, you are actually learning more about the value of your degree. What's important in your search at this point is not to become critical or selective but rather to develop as long a list of possibilities as you can. Every source used will help you add new and potentially exciting jobs to your growing list.

Classified Ads

It has been well publicized that the classified ad section of the newspaper represents only a small fraction of the current job market. Nevertheless, the weekly classified ads can be a great help to you in your search. Although they may not be the best place to look for a job, they can teach you a lot about the job market. Classified ads provide a good education in job descriptions, duties, responsibilities, and qualifications. In addition, they provide insight into which industries are actively recruiting and some indication of the area's employment market. This is particularly helpful when seeking a position in a specific geographic area and/or a specific field. For your purposes, classified ads are a good source for job titles to add to your list.

Read the Sunday classified ads in a major market newspaper for several weeks in a row. Cut and paste all the ads that interest you and seem to call for something close to your education, skills, experience, and interests.

Remember that classified ads are written for what an organization *hopes* to find; you don't have to meet absolutely every criterion. However, if certain requirements are stated as absolute minimums and you cannot meet them, it's best not to waste your time and that of the employer.

The weekly classified want ads exercise is important because these jobs are out in the marketplace. They truly exist, and people with your qualifications are being sought to apply. What's more, many of these advertisements describe the duties and responsibilities of the job advertised and give you a beginning sense of the challenges and opportunities such a position presents. Some will indicate salary, and that will be helpful as well. This information will better define the jobs for you and provide some good material for possible interviews in that field.

Explore Job Descriptions

Once you've arrived at a solid list of possible job titles that interest you and for which you believe you are somewhat qualified, it's a good idea to do some research on each of these jobs. The preeminent source for such job information is the *Dictionary of Occupational Titles*, or *DOT* (wave.net/upg/immigration/dot_index.html). This directory lists every conceivable job and provides excellent up-to-date information on duties and responsibilities, interactions with associates, and day-to-day assignments and tasks. These descriptions provide a thorough job analysis, but they do not consider the possible employers or the environments in which a job may be performed. So, although a position as public relations officer may be well defined in terms of duties and responsibilities, it does not explain the differences in doing public relations work in a college or a hospital or a factory or a bank. You will need to look somewhere else for work settings.

Learn More About Possible Work Settings

After reading some job descriptions, you may choose to edit and revise your list of job titles once again, discarding those you feel are not suitable and keeping those that continue to hold your interest. Or you may wish to keep your list intact and see where these jobs may be located. For example, if you are interested in public relations and you appear to have those skills and the requisite education, you'll want to know which organizations do public relations. How can you find that out? How much income does someone in public relations make a year and what is the employment potential for the field of public relations?

To answer these and many other questions about your list of job titles, we recommend you try any of the following resources: *Careers Encyclopedia*, the professional societies and resources found throughout this book, *College to Career: The Guide to Job Opportunities*, and the *Occupational Outlook Handbook* (http://stats.bls.gov/ocohome.htm). Each of these resources, in a different way, will help to put the job titles you have selected into an employer context. Perhaps the most extensive discussion is found in the *Occupational Outlook Handbook*, which gives a thorough presentation of the nature of the work, the working conditions, employment statistics, training, other qualifications, and advancement possibilities as well as job outlook and earnings. Related occupations are also detailed, and a select bibliography is provided to help you find additional information.

Continuing with our public relations example, your search through these reference materials would teach you that the public relations jobs you find attractive are available in larger hospitals, financial institutions, most corporations (both consumer goods and industrial goods), media organizations, and colleges and universities.

Networking

Networking is the process of deliberately establishing relationships to get career-related information or to alert potential employers that you are available for work. Networking is critically important to today's job seeker for two reasons: it will help you get the information you need, and it can help you find out about *all* of the available jobs.

Get the Information You Need

Networkers will review your résumé and give you feedback on its effectiveness. They will talk about the job you are looking for and give you a candid appraisal of how they see your strengths and weaknesses. If they have a good sense of the industry or the employment sector for that job, you'll get their feelings on future trends in the industry as well. Some networkers will be very forthcoming about salaries, job-hunting techniques, and suggestions for your job search strategy. Many have been known to place calls right from the interview desk to friends and associates who might be interested in you.

Each networker will make his or her own contribution, and each will be valuable.

Because organizations must evolve to adapt to current global market needs, the information provided by decision makers within various organizations will be critical to your success as a new job market entrant. For example, you might learn about the concept of virtual organizations from a networker. Virtual organizations coordinate economic activity to deliver value to customers by using resources outside the traditional boundaries of the organization. This concept is being discussed and implemented by chief executive officers of many organizations, including Ford Motor, Dell, and IBM. Networking can help you find out about this and other trends currently affecting the industries under your consideration.

Find Out About All of the Available Jobs

Not every job that is available at this very moment is advertised for potential applicants to see. This is called the *hidden job market*. Only 15 to 20 percent of all jobs are formally advertised, which means that 80 to 85 percent of available jobs do not appear in published channels. Networking will help you become more knowledgeable about all the employment opportunities available during your job search period.

Although someone you might talk to today doesn't know of any openings within his or her organization, tomorrow or next week or next month an opening may occur. If you've taken the time to show an interest in and knowledge of their organization, if you've shown the company representative how you can help achieve organizational goals and that you can fit into the organization, you'll be one of the first candidates considered for the position.

Networking: A Proactive Approach

Networking is a proactive rather than a reactive approach. You, as a job seeker, are expected to initiate a certain level of activity on your own behalf; you cannot afford to simply respond to jobs listed in the newspaper. Being proactive means building a network of contacts that includes informed and interested decision makers who will provide you with up-to-date knowledge of the current job market and increase your chances of finding out about employment opportunities appropriate for your interests, experience, and level of education. An old axiom of networking says, "You are only two phone calls away from the information you need." In other words, by talking to enough people, you will quickly come across someone who can offer you help.

Preparing to Network

In deliberately establishing relationships, maximize your efforts by organizing your approach. Five specific areas in which you can organize your efforts include reviewing your self-assessment, reviewing your research on job sites and organizations, deciding who you want to talk to, keeping track of all your efforts, and creating your self-promotion tools.

Review Your Self-Assessment

Your self-assessment is as important a tool in preparing to network as it has been in other aspects of your job search. You have carefully evaluated your personal traits, personal values, economic needs, longer-term goals, skill base, preferred skills, and underdeveloped skills. During the networking process you will be called upon to communicate what you know about yourself and relate it to the information or job you seek. Be sure to review the exercises that you completed in the self-assessment section of this book in preparation for networking. We've explained that you need to assess which skills you have acquired from your major that are of general value to an employer; be ready to express those in ways he or she can appreciate as useful in the organizations.

Review Research on Job Sites and Organizations

In addition, individuals assisting you will expect that you'll have at least some background information on the occupation or industry of interest to you. Refer to the appropriate sections of this book and other relevant publications to acquire the background information necessary for effective networking. They'll explain how to identify not only the job titles that might be of interest to you but also which kinds of organizations employ people to do that job. You will develop some sense of working conditions and expectations about duties and responsibilities—all of which will be of help in your networking interviews.

Decide Whom You Want to Talk To

Networking cannot begin until you decide who you want to talk to and, in general, what type of information you hope to gain from your contacts. Once you know this, it's time to begin developing a list of contacts. Five useful sources for locating contacts are described here.

College Alumni Network. Most colleges and universities have created a formal network of alumni and friends of the institution who are particularly interested in helping currently enrolled students and graduates of their alma mater gain employment-related information.

It is usually a simple process to make use of an alumni network. Visit your college's website and locate the alumni office and/or your career center. Either or both sites will have information about your school's alumni network. You'll be provided with information on shadowing experiences, geographic information, or those alumni offering job referrals. If you don't find what you're looking for, don't hesitate to phone or e-mail your career center and ask what they can do to help you connect with an alum.

Alumni networkers may provide some combination of the following services: day-long shadowing experiences, telephone interviews, in-person interviews, information on relocating to given geographic areas, internship information, suggestions on graduate school study, and job vacancy notices.

Present and Former Supervisors. If you believe you are on good terms with present or former job supervisors, they may be an excellent resource for providing information or directing you to appropriate resources that would have information related to your current interests and needs. Additionally, these supervisors probably belong to professional organizations that they might be willing to utilize to get information for you.

Employers in Your Area. Although you may be interested in working in a geographic location different from the one where you currently reside, don't overlook the value of the knowledge and contacts those around you are able to provide. Use the local telephone directory and newspaper to identify the types of organizations you are thinking of working for or professionals who have the kinds of jobs you are interested in. Recently, a call made to a local hospital's financial administrator for information on working in health-care financial administration yielded more pertinent information on training seminars, regional professional organizations, and potential employment sites than a national organization was willing to provide.

Employers in Geographic Areas Where You Hope to Work. If you are thinking about relocating, identifying prospective employers or informational contacts in the new location will be critical to your success. Here are some tips for online searching. First, use a "metasearch" engine to get the most out of your search. Metasearch engines combine several engines into one powerful tool. We frequently use dogpile.com and metasearch.com for this purpose. Try using the city and state as your keywords in a search. *New Haven, Connecticut* will bring you to the city's website with links to the chamber of commerce, member businesses, and other valuable resources. By using looksmart.com you can locate newspapers in any area, and they, too, can provide valuable insight before you relocate. Of course, both dogpile and metasearch can lead you to yellow and white page directories in areas you are considering.

Professional Associations and Organizations. Professional associations and organizations can provide valuable information in several areas: career paths that you might not have considered, qualifications relating to those career choices, publications that list current job openings, and workshops or seminars that will enhance your professional knowledge and skills. They can also be excellent sources for background information on given industries: their health, current problems, and future challenges.

There are several excellent resources available to help you locate professional associations and organizations that would have information to meet your needs. Two especially useful publications are the *Encyclopedia of Associations* and *National Trade and Professional Associations of the United States*.

Keep Track of All Your Efforts

It can be difficult, almost impossible, to remember all the details related to each contact you make during the networking process, so you will want to develop a record-keeping system that works for you. Formalize this process by using your computer to keep a record of the people and organizations you want to contact. You can simply record the contact's name, address, and telephone number, and what information you hope to gain.

You could record this as a simple Word document and you could still use the "Find" function if you were trying to locate some data and could only recall the firm's name or the contact's name. If you're comfortable with database management and you have some database software on your computer, then you can put information at your fingertips even if you have only the zip code! The point here is not technological sophistication but good record keeping.

Once you have created this initial list, it will be helpful to keep more detailed information as you begin to actually make the contacts. Those details should include complete contact information, the date and content of each contact, names and information for additional networkers, and required follow-up. Don't forget to send a letter thanking your contact for his or her time! Your contact will appreciate your recall of details of your meetings and conversations, and the information will help you to focus your networking efforts.

Create Your Self-Promotion Tools

There are two types of promotional tools that are used in the networking process. The first is a résumé and cover letter, and the second is a one-minute "infomercial," which may be given over the telephone or in person.

Techniques for writing an effective résumé and cover letter are discussed in Chapter 2. Once you have reviewed that material and prepared these important documents, you will have created one of your self-promotion tools.

The one-minute infomercial will demand that you begin tying your interests, abilities, and skills to the people or organizations you want to network with. Think about your goal for making the contact to help you understand what you should say about yourself. You should be able to express yourself easily and convincingly. If, for example, you are contacting an alumnus of your institution to obtain the names of possible employment sites in a distant city, be prepared to discuss why you are interested in moving to that location, the types of jobs you are interested in, and the skills and abilities you possess that will make you a qualified candidate.

To create a meaningful one-minute infomercial, write it out, practice it as if it will be a spoken presentation, rewrite it, and practice it again if necessary until expressing yourself comes easily and is convincing.

Here's a simplified example of an infomercial for use over the telephone:

Hello, Dr. Frank? My name is Jordan Stoll and I am a recent graduate of the University of Michigan. I was a biomedical engineering major and I possess many of the skills that are valued in the healthcare industry, including analytical and research skills, as well as community outreach experience.

I know you're extremely busy, so I'll get to the point. I'm calling today because I would like to gather more information about the work biomedical engineers do in the healthcare field to make sure that I'm making the best career choice for me. I'm hoping you'll have some time to sit down with me for about half an hour and discuss your perspective on biomedical engineeering careers. Would you be willing to do that for me?

I would greatly appreciate any time you're able to offer me. I am available most mornings, if that's good for you.

It very well may happen that your employer contact wishes you to communicate by e-mail. The infomercial quoted above could easily be rewritten for an e-mail message. You should "cut and paste" your résumé right into the e-mail text itself.

Other effective self-promotion tools include portfolios for those in the arts, writing professions, or teaching. Portfolios show examples of work, photographs of projects or classroom activities, or certificates and credentials that are job related. There may not be an opportunity to use the portfolio during an interview, and it is not something that should be left with the organization. It is designed to be explained and displayed by the creator. However, during some networking meetings, there may be an opportunity to illustrate a point or strengthen a qualification by exhibiting the portfolio.

Beginning the Networking Process

Set the Tone for Your Communications

It can be useful to establish "tone words" for any communications you embark upon. Before making your first telephone call or writing your first letter, decide what you want the person to think of you. If you are networking to try to obtain a job, your tone words might include descriptors such as *genuine*, *informed*, and *self-knowledgeable*. When you're trying to acquire information, your tone words may have a slightly different focus, such as *courteous*, *organized*, *focused*, and *well-spoken*. Use the tone words you establish for your contacts to guide you through the networking process.

Honestly Express Your Intentions

When contacting individuals, it is important to be honest about your reasons for making the contact. Establish your purpose in your own mind and be able and ready to articulate it concisely. Determine an initial agenda, whether it be informational questioning or self-promotion, present it to your contact, and be ready to respond immediately. If you don't adequately prepare before initiating your overture, you may find yourself at a disadvantage if you're asked to immediately begin your informational interview or self-promotion during the first phone conversation or visit.

Start Networking Within Your Circle of Confidence

Once you have organized your approach—by utilizing specific researching methods, creating a system for keeping track of the people you will contact, and developing effective self-promotion tools—you are ready to begin networking. The best way to begin networking is by talking with a group of people you trust and feel comfortable with. This group is usually made up of your family, friends, and career counselors. No matter who is in this inner circle, they will have a special interest in seeing you succeed in your job search. In addition, because they will be easy to talk to, you should try taking some risks in terms of practicing your information-seeking approach. Gain confidence in talking about the strengths you bring to an organization and the underdeveloped skills you feel hinder your candidacy. Be sure to review the section on self-assessment for tips on approaching each of these areas. Ask for critical but constructive feedback from the people in your circle of confidence on the letters you write and the one-minute infomercial you have developed. Evaluate whether you want to make the changes they suggest, then practice the changes on others within this circle.

Stretch the Boundaries of Your Networking Circle of Confidence

Once you have refined the promotional tools you will use to accomplish your networking goals, you will want to make additional contacts. Because you will not know most of these people, it will be a less comfortable activity to undertake. The practice that you gained with your inner circle of trusted friends should have prepared you to now move outside of that comfort zone.

It is said that any information a person needs is only two phone calls away, but the information cannot be gained until you (1) make a reasonable guess about who might have the information you need and (2) pick up the telephone to make the call. Using your network list that includes alumni, instructors, supervisors, employers, and associations, you can begin preparing your list of questions that will allow you to get the information you need.

Prepare the Questions You Want to Ask

Networkers can provide you with the insider's perspective on any given field and you can ask them questions that you might not want to ask in an interview. For example, you can ask them to describe the more repetitious or mundane parts of the job or ask them for a realistic idea of salary expectations. Be sure to prepare your questions ahead of time so that you are organized and efficient.

Be Prepared to Answer Some Questions

To communicate effectively, you must anticipate questions that will be asked of you by the networkers you contact. Revisit the self-assessment process you undertook and the research you've done so that you can effortlessly respond to questions about your short- and long-term goals and the kinds of jobs you are most interested in pursuing.

General Networking Tips

Make Every Contact Count. Setting the tone for each interaction is critical. Approaches that will help you communicate in an effective way include politeness, being appreciative of time provided to you, and being prepared and thorough. Remember, *everyone* within an organization has a circle of influence, so be prepared to interact effectively with each person you encounter in the networking process, including secretarial and support staff. Many information or job seekers have thwarted their own efforts by being rude to some individuals they encountered as they networked because they made the incorrect assumption that certain persons were unimportant.

Sometimes your contacts may be surprised at their ability to help you. After meeting and talking with you, they might think they have not offered much in the way of help. A day or two later, however, they may make a contact that would be useful to you and refer you to that person.

With Each Contact, Widen Your Circle of Networkers. Always leave an informational interview with the names of at least two more people who can help you get the information or job that you are seeking. Don't be shy about asking for additional contacts; networking is all about increasing the number of people you can interact with to achieve your goals.

Make Your Own Decisions. As you talk with different people and get answers to the questions you pose, you may hear conflicting information or get conflicting suggestions. Your job is to listen to these "experts" and decide what information and which suggestions will help you achieve *your* goals. Only implement those suggestions that you believe will work for you.

Shutting Down Your Network

As you achieve the goals that motivated your networking activity—getting the information you need or the job you want—the time will come to inactivate all or parts of your network. As you do, be sure to tell your primary supporters about your change in status. Call or write to each one of them and give them as many details about your new status as you feel is necessary to maintain a positive relationship.

Because a network takes on a life of its own, activity undertaken on your behalf will continue even after you cease your efforts. As you get calls or are contacted in some fashion, be sure to inform these networkers about your change in status, and thank them for assistance they have provided.

Information on the latest employment trends indicates that workers will change jobs or careers several times in their lifetime. Networking, then, will be a critical aspect in the span of your professional life. If you carefully and thoughtfully conduct your networking activities during your job search, you will have a solid foundation of experience when you need to network the next time around.

Where Are These Jobs, Anyway?

Having a list of job titles that you've designed around your own career interests and skills is an excellent beginning. It means you've really thought about who you are and what you are presenting to the employment market. It has caused you to think seriously about the most appealing environments to work in, and you have identified some employer types that represent these environments.

The research and the thinking that you've done thus far will be used again and again. They will be helpful in writing your résumé and cover letters, in talking about yourself on the telephone to prospective employers, and in answering interview questions.

Now is a good time to begin to narrow the field of job titles and employment sites down to some specific employers to initiate the employment contact.

Find Out Which Employers Hire People Like You

This section will provide tips, techniques, and specific resources for developing an actual list of specific employers that can be used to make contacts. It is only an outline that you must be prepared to tailor to your own particular needs and according to what you bring to the job search. Once again, it is important to communicate with others along the way exactly what you're looking for and what your goals are for the research you're doing. Librarians, employers, career counselors, friends, friends of friends, business contacts, and bookstore staff will all have helpful information on geographically specific and new resources to aid you in locating employers who'll hire you.

Identify Information Resources

Your interview wardrobe and your new résumé might have put a dent in your wallet, but the resources you'll need to pursue your job search are available for free. The categories of information detailed here are not hard to find and are yours for the browsing.

Numerous resources described in this section will help you identify actual employers. Use all of them or any others that you identify as available in your geographic area. As you become experienced in this process, you'll quickly figure out which information sources are helpful and which are not. If you live in a rural area, a well-planned day trip to a major city that includes a college career office, a large college or city library, state and federal employment centers, a chamber of commerce office, and a well-stocked bookstore can produce valuable results.

There are many excellent resources available to help you identify actual job sites. They are categorized into employer directories (usually indexed by product lines and geographic location), geographically based directories (designed to highlight particular cities, regions, or states), career-specific directories (e.g., *Sports MarketPlace*, which lists tens of thousands of firms involved with sports), periodicals and newspapers, targeted job posting publications, and videos. This is by no means meant to be a complete treatment of resources but rather a starting point for identifying useful resources.

Working from the more general references to highly specific resources, we provide a basic list to help you begin your search. Many of these you'll find easily available. In some cases reference librarians and others will suggest even better materials for your particular situation. Start to create your own customized bibliography of job search references.

Geographically Based Directories. The Job Bank series published by Bob Adams, Inc. (aip.com) contains detailed entries on each area's major employers, including business activity, address, phone number, and hiring contact name. Many listings specify educational backgrounds being sought in potential employees. Each volume contains a solid discussion of each city's or state's major employment sectors. Organizations are also indexed by industry. Job Bank volumes are available for the following places: Atlanta, Boston, Chicago, Dallas–Ft. Worth, Denver, Detroit, Florida, Houston, Los Angeles, Minneapolis, New York, Ohio, Philadelphia, San Francisco, Seattle, St. Louis, Washington, D.C., and other cities throughout the Northwest.

National Job Bank (careercity.com) lists employers in every state, along with contact names and commonly hired job categories. Included are many small companies often overlooked by other directories. Companies are also indexed by industry. This publication provides information on educational backgrounds sought and lists company benefits.

Periodicals and Newspapers. Several sources are available to help you locate which journals or magazines carry job advertisements in your field. Other resources help you identify opportunities in other parts of the country.

- *Where the Jobs Are: A Comprehensive Directory of 1200 Journals Listing Career Opportunities*
- *Corptech Fast 5000 Company Locator*
- *National Ad Search* (nationaladsearch.com)
- *The Federal Jobs Digest* (jobsfed.com) and *Federal Career Opportunities*
- *World Chamber of Commerce Directory* (chamberofcommerce.org)

This list is certainly not exhaustive; use it to begin your job search work.

Targeted Job Posting Publications. Although the resources that follow are national in scope, they are either targeted to one medium of contact (telephone), focused on specific types of jobs, or less comprehensive than the sources previously listed.

- Careers.org (careers.org/index.html)
- *The Job Hunter* (jobhunter.com)
- *Current Jobs for Graduates* (graduatejobs.com)
- *Environmental Opportunities* (ecojobs.com)
- *Y National Vacancy List* (ymca.net/employment/ymca_recruiting/ jobright.htm)
- *ArtSEARCH*
- *Community Jobs*
- *National Association of Colleges and Employers: Job Choices series*
- *National Association of Colleges and Employers* (jobweb.com)

Videos. You may be one of the many job seekers who likes to get information via a medium other than paper. Many career libraries, public libraries, and career centers in libraries carry an assortment of videos that will help you learn new techniques and get information helpful in the job search.

Locate Information Resources
Throughout these introductory chapters, we have continually referred you to various websites for information on everything from job listings to career information. Using the Web gives you a mobility at your computer that you don't enjoy if you rely solely on books or newspapers or printed journals.

Moreover, material on the Web, if the site is maintained, can be the most up-to-date information available.

You'll eventually identify the information resources that work best for you, but make certain you've covered the full range of resources before you begin to rely on a smaller list. Here's a short list of informational sites that many job seekers find helpful:

- Public and college libraries
- College career centers
- Bookstores
- The Internet
- Local and state government personnel offices
- Career/job fairs

Each one of these sites offers a collection of resources that will help you get the information you need.

As you meet and talk with service professionals at all these sites, be sure to let them know what you're doing. Inform them of your job search, what you've already accomplished, and what you're looking for. The more people who know you're job seeking, the greater the possibility that someone will have information or know someone who can help you along your way.

4

Interviewing and Job Offer Considerations

Certainly, there can be no one part of the job search process more fraught with anxiety and worry than the interview. Yet seasoned job seekers welcome the interview and will often say, "Just get me an interview and I'm on my way!" They understand that the interview is crucial to the hiring process and equally crucial for them, as job candidates, to have the opportunity of a personal dialogue to add to what the employer may already have learned from the résumé, cover letter, and telephone conversations.

Believe it or not, the interview is to be welcomed, and even enjoyed! It is a perfect opportunity for you, the candidate, to sit down with an employer and express yourself and display who you are and what you want. Of course, it takes thought and planning and a little strategy; after all, it *is* a job interview! But it can be a positive, if not pleasant, experience and one you can look back on and feel confident about your performance and effort.

For many new job seekers, a job, any job, seems a wonderful thing. But seasoned interview veterans know that the job interview is an important step for both sides—the employer and the candidate—to see what each has to offer and whether there is going to be a "fit" of personalities, work styles, and attitudes. And it is this concept of balance in the interview, that both sides have important parts to play, that holds the key to success in mastering this aspect of the job search strategy.

Try to think of the interview as a conversation between two interested and equal partners. You both have important, even vital, information to deliver and to learn. Of course, there's no denying the employer has some leverage, especially in the initial interview for recruitment or any interview scheduled by the candidate and not the recruiter. That should not prevent the interviewee from seeking to play an equal part in what should be a fair

55

exchange of information. Too often the untutored candidate allows the interview to become one-sided. The employer asks all the questions and the candidate simply responds. The ideal would be for two mutually interested parties to sit down and discuss possibilities for each. This is a conversation of significance, and it requires preparation, thought about the tone of the interview, and planning of the nature and details of the information to be exchanged.

Preparing for the Interview

The length of most initial interviews is about thirty minutes. Given the brevity, the information that is exchanged ought to be important. The candidate should be delivering material that the employer cannot discover on the résumé, and in turn, the candidate should be learning things about the employer that he or she could not otherwise find out. After all, if you have only thirty minutes, why waste time on information that is already published? The information exchanged is more than just factual, and both sides will learn much from what they see of each other, as well. How the candidate looks, speaks, and acts are important to the employer. The employer's attention to the interview and awareness of the candidate's résumé, the setting, and the quality of information presented are important to the candidate.

Just as the employer has every right to be disappointed when a prospect is late for the interview, looks unkempt, and seems ill-prepared to answer fairly standard questions, the candidate may be disappointed with an interviewer who isn't ready for the meeting, hasn't learned the basic résumé facts, and is constantly interrupted by telephone calls. In either situation there's good reason to feel let down.

There are many elements to a successful interview, and some of them are not easy to describe or prepare for. Sometimes there is just a chemistry between interviewer and interviewee that brings out the best in both, and a good exchange takes place. But there is much the candidate can do to pave the way for success in terms of his or her résumé, personal appearance, goals, and interview strategy—each of which we will discuss. However, none of this preparation is as important as the time and thought the candidate gives to personal self-assessment.

Self-Assessment
Neither a stunning résumé nor an expensive, well-tailored suit can compensate for candidates who do not know what they want, where they are going, or why they are interviewing with a particular employer. Self-assessment, the

process by which we begin to know and acknowledge our own particular blend of education, experiences, needs, and goals, is not something that can be sorted out the weekend before a major interview. Of all the elements of interview preparation, this one requires the longest lead time and cannot be faked.

Because the time allotted for most interviews is brief, it is all the more important for job candidates to understand and express succinctly why they are there and what they have to offer. This is not a time for undue modesty (or for braggadocio either); it is a time for a compelling, reasoned statement of why you feel that you and this employer might make a good match. It means you have to have thought about your skills, interests, and attributes; related those to your life experiences and your own history of challenges and opportunities; and determined what that indicates about your strengths, preferences, values, and areas needing further development.

If you need some assistance with self-assessment issues, refer to Chapter 1. Included are suggested exercises that can be done as needed, such as making up an experiential diary and extracting obvious strengths and weaknesses from past experiences. These simple assignments will help you look at past activities as collections of tasks with accompanying skills and responsibilities. Don't overlook your high school or college career office. Many offer personal counseling on self-assessment issues and may provide testing instruments such as the *Myers-Briggs Type Indicator (MBTI)*, the *Harrington-O'Shea Career Decision-Making System (CDM)*, the *Strong Interest Inventory (SII)*, or any other of a wide selection of assessment tools that can help you clarify some of these issues prior to the interview stage of your job search.

The Résumé

Résumé preparation has been discussed in detail, and some basic examples were provided. In this section we want to concentrate on how best to use your résumé in the interview. In most cases the employer will have seen the résumé prior to the interview, and, in fact, it may well have been the quality of that résumé that secured the interview opportunity.

An interview is a conversation, however, and not an exercise in reading. So, if the employer hasn't seen your résumé and you have brought it along to the interview, wait until asked or until the end of the interview to offer it. Otherwise, you may find yourself staring at the back of your résumé and simply answering "yes" and "no" to a series of questions drawn from that document.

Sometimes an interviewer is not prepared and does not know or recall the contents of the résumé and may use the résumé to a greater or lesser degree as a "prompt" during the interview. It is for you to judge what that may indicate about the individual performing the interview or the employer. If your interviewer seems surprised by the scheduled meeting, relies on the résumé to an inordinate degree, and seems otherwise unfamiliar with your background, this lack of preparation for the hiring process could well be a symptom of general management disorganization or may simply be the result of poor planning on the part of one individual. It is your responsibility as a potential employee to be aware of these signals and make your decisions accordingly.

It is perfectly acceptable for you to guide the conversation back to a more interpersonal style by saying, "Ms. Smith, you might be interested in some recent research experience I gained through an internship that is not detailed on my résumé." This strategy might give you an opportunity to convey more information about your strengths and weaknesses and to reengage the direction of your interview.

By all means, bring at least one copy of your résumé to the interview. Occasionally, at the close of an interview, an interviewer will express an interest in circulating a résumé to several departments, and you could then offer the copy you brought. Sometimes, an interview appointment provides an opportunity to meet others in the organization who may express an interest in you and your background, and it may be helpful to follow up with a copy of your résumé. Our best advice, however, is to keep it out of sight until needed or requested.

Employer Information
Whether your interview is for graduate school admission, an overseas corporate position, or a position with a local company, it is important to know something about the employer or the organization. Keeping in mind that the interview is relatively brief and that you will hopefully have other interviews with other organizations, it is important to keep your research in proportion. If secondary interviews are called for, you will have additional time to do further research. For the first interview, it is helpful to know the organization's mission, goals, size, scope of operations, and so forth. Your research may uncover recent areas of challenge or particular successes that may help to fuel the interview. Use the "What Do They Call the Job You Want?" section of Chapter 3, your library, and your career or guidance office to help

you locate this information in the most efficient way possible. Don't be shy in asking advice of these counseling and guidance professionals on how best to spend your preparation time. With some practice, you'll soon learn how much information is enough and which kinds of information are most useful to you.

Interview Content

We've already discussed how it can help to think of the interview as an important conversation—one that, as with any conversation, you want to find pleasant and interesting and to leave you with a good feeling. But because this conversation is especially important, the information that's exchanged is critical to its success. What do you want them to know about you? What do you need to know about them? What interview technique do you need to particularly pay attention to? How do you want to manage the close of the interview? What steps will follow in the hiring process?

Except for the professional interviewer, most of us find interviewing stressful and anxiety-provoking. Developing a strategy before you begin interviewing will help you relieve some stress and anxiety. One particular strategy that has worked for many and may work for you is interviewing by objective. Before you interview, write down three to five goals you would like to achieve for that interview. They may be technique goals: smile a little more, have a firmer handshake, be sure to ask about the next stage in the interview process before leaving. They may be content-oriented goals: find out about the company's current challenges and opportunities; be sure to speak of your recent research, writing experiences, or foreign travel. Whatever your goals, jot down a few of them as goals for each interview.

Most people find that in trying to achieve these few goals, their interviewing technique becomes more organized and focused. After the interview, the most common question friends and family ask is "How did it go?" With this technique, you have an indication of whether you met *your* goals for the meeting, not just some vague idea of how it went. Chances are, if you accomplished what you wanted to, it improved the quality of the entire interview. As you continue to interview, you will want to revise your goals to continue improving your interview skills.

Now, add to the concept of the significant conversation the idea of a beginning, a middle, and a closing and you will have two thoughts that will give your interview a distinctive character. Be sure to make your introduction warm and cordial. Say your full name (and if it's a difficult-to-pronounce name, help the interviewer to pronounce it) and make certain you know your interviewer's name and how to pronounce it. Most interviews begin with some "soft talk" about the weather, chat about the candidate's trip to the interview site, or national events. This is done as a courtesy to relax both you and the interviewer, to get you talking, and to generally try to defuse the atmosphere of excessive tension. Try to be yourself, engage in the conversation, and don't try to second-guess the interviewer. This is simply what it appears to be—casual conversation.

Once you and the interviewer move on to exchange more serious information in the middle part of the interview, the two most important concerns become your ability to handle challenging questions and your success at asking meaningful ones. Interviewer questions will probably fall into one of three categories: personal assessment and career direction, academic assessment, and knowledge of the employer. Here are a few examples of questions in each category:

Personal Assessment and Career Direction
1. What motivates you to put forth your best effort?
2. What do you consider to be your greatest strengths and weaknesses?
3. What qualifications do you have that make you think you will be successful in this career?

Academic Assessment
1. What led you to choose your major?
2. What subjects did you like best and least? Why?
3. How has your college experience prepared you for this career?

Knowledge of the Employer
1. What do you think it takes to be successful in an organization like ours?
2. In what ways do you think you can make a contribution to our organization?
3. Why did you choose to seek a position with this organization?

The interviewer wants a response to each question but is also gauging your enthusiasm, preparedness, and willingness to communicate. In each response you should provide some information about yourself that can be related to the employer's needs. A common mistake is to give too much information. Answer each question completely, but be careful not to run on too long with extensive details or examples.

Questions About Underdeveloped Skills

Most employers interview people who have met some minimum criteria of education and experience. They interview candidates to see who they are, to learn what kind of personality they exhibit, and to get some sense of how they might fit into the existing organization. It may be that you are asked about skills the employer hopes to find and that you have not documented. Maybe it's statistical process control, experience with a specific simulation software tool, or knowledge of program controls strategies.

To questions about skills and experiences you don't have, answer honestly and forthrightly and try to offer some additional information about skills you do have. For example, perhaps the employer is disappointed you have no lean production experience. An honest answer may be as follows:

> *No, unfortunately, I do understand lean principles. I attended a short course on the subject during my internship with Smith Manufacturing and did an independent study with Professor Jones on Toyota's production methodology. I think I could get up on the learning curve quickly.*

The employer hears an honest admission of lack of experience but is reassured by some specific skill details that do relate to grant writing and a confident manner that suggests enthusiasm and interest in a challenge.

For many students, questions about their possible contribution to an employer's organization can prove challenging. Because your education has probably not included specific training for a job, you need to review your academic record and select capabilities you have developed in your major that an employer can appreciate. For example, perhaps you read well and can analyze and condense what you've read into smaller, more focused pieces. That could be valuable. Or maybe you did some serious research and you know you have valuable investigative skills. Your public speaking might be highly developed and you might use visual aids appropriately and effectively. Or maybe your skill at correspondence, memos, and messages is effective. Whatever it is, you must take it out of the academic context and put it into a new, employer-friendly context so your interviewer can best judge how you could help the organization.

Exhibiting knowledge of the organization will, without a doubt, show the interviewer that you are interested enough in the available position to have done some legwork in preparation for the interview. Remember, it is not necessary to know every detail of the organization's history but rather to have a general knowledge about why it is in business and how the industry is faring.

Sometime during the interview, generally after the midway point, you'll be asked if you have any questions for the interviewer. Your questions will tell the employer much about your attitude and your desire to understand the organization's expectations so you can compare them to your own strengths. The following are just a few questions you might want to ask:

1. What is the communication style of the organization? (meetings, memos, and so forth)
2. What would a typical day in this position be like for me?
3. What have been some of the interesting challenges and opportunities your organization has recently faced?

Most interviews draw to a natural closing point, so be careful not to prolong the discussion. At a signal from the interviewer, wind up your presentation, express your appreciation for the opportunity, and be sure to ask what the next stage in the process will be. When can you expect to hear from them? Will they be conducting second-tier interviews? If you are interested and haven't heard, would they mind a phone call? Be sure to collect a business card with the name and phone number of your interviewer. On your way out, you might have an opportunity to pick up organizational literature you haven't seen before.

With the right preparation—a thorough self-assessment, professional clothing, and employer information—you'll be able to set and achieve the goals you have established for the interview process.

Interview Follow-Up

Quite often there is a considerable time lag between interviewing for a position and being hired or, in the case of the networker, between your phone call or letter to a possible contact and the opportunity of a meeting. This can be frustrating. "Why aren't they contacting me?" "I thought I'd get another interview, but no one has telephoned." "Am I out of the running?" You don't know what is happening.

Consider the Differing Perspectives

Of course, there is another perspective—that of the networker or hiring organization. Organizations are complex, with multiple tasks that need to be accomplished each day. Hiring is a discrete activity that does not occur as frequently as other job assignments. The hiring process might have to take second place to other, more immediate organizational needs. Although it may be very important to you, and it is certainly ultimately significant to the employer, other issues such as fiscal management, planning and product development, employer vacation periods, or financial constraints may prevent an organization or individual within that organization from acting on your employment or your request for information as quickly as you or they would prefer.

Use Your Communications Skills

Good communication is essential here to resolve any anxieties, and the responsibility is on you, the job or information seeker. Too many job seekers and networkers offer as an excuse that they don't want to "bother" the organization by writing letters or calling. Let us assure you here and now, once and for all, that if you are troubling an organization by over-communicating, someone will indicate that situation to you quite clearly. If not, you can only assume you are a worthwhile prospect and the employer appreciates being reminded of your availability and interest. Let's look at follow-up practices in the job interview process and the networking situation separately.

Following Up on the Employment Interview

A brief thank-you note following an interview is an excellent and polite way to begin a series of follow-up communications with a potential employer with whom you have interviewed and want to remain in touch. It should be just that—a thank-you for a good meeting. If you failed to mention some fact or experience during your interview that you think might add to your candidacy, you may use this note to do that. However, this should be essentially a note whose overall tone is appreciative and, if appropriate, indicative of a continuing interest in pursuing any opportunity that may exist with that organization. It is one of the few pieces of business correspondence that may be handwritten, but always use plain, good-quality, standard-size paper.

If, however, at this point you are no longer interested in the employer, the thank-you note is an appropriate time to indicate that. You are under no obligation to identify any reason for not continuing to pursue employment with that organization, but if you are so inclined to indicate your professional reasons (pursuing other employers more akin to your interests, looking for greater income production than this employer can provide, a different geographic location), you certainly may. It should not be written with an eye to negotiation, for it will not be interpreted as such.

As part of your interview closing, you should have taken the initiative to establish lines of communication for continuing information about your candidacy. If you asked permission to telephone, wait a week following your thank-you note, then telephone your contact simply to inquire how things are progressing on your employment status. The feedback you receive here should be taken at face value. If your interviewer simply has no information, he or she will tell you so and indicate whether you should call again and when. Don't be discouraged if this should continue over some period of time.

If during this time something occurs that you think improves or changes your candidacy (some new qualification or experience you may have had), including any offers from other organizations, by all means telephone or write to inform the employer about this. In the case of an offer from a competing but less desirable or equally desirable organization, telephone your contact, explain what has happened, express your real interest in the organization, and inquire whether some determination on your employment might be made before you must respond to this other offer. An organization that is truly interested in you may be moved to make a decision about your candidacy. Equally possible is the scenario in which they are not yet ready to make a decision and so advise you to take the offer that has been presented. Again, you have no ethical alternative but to deal with the information presented in a straightforward manner.

When accepting other employment, be sure to contact any employers still actively considering you and inform them of your new job. Thank them graciously for their consideration. There are many other job seekers out there just like you who will benefit from having their candidacy improved when others bow out of the race. Who knows, you might at some future time have occasion to interact professionally with one of the organizations with which you sought employment. How embarrassing it would be to have someone remember you as the candidate who failed to notify them that you were taking a job elsewhere!

In all of your follow-up communications, keep good notes of whom you spoke with, when you called, and any instructions that were given about return communications. This will prevent any misunderstandings and provide you with good records of what has transpired.

Job Offer Considerations

For many recent college graduates, the thrill of their first job and, for some, the most substantial regular income they have ever earned seems an excess of good fortune coming at once. To question that first income or to be critical in any way of the conditions of employment at the time of the initial offer seems like looking a gift horse in the mouth. It doesn't seem to occur to many new hires even to attempt to negotiate any aspect of their first job. And, as many employers who deal with entry-level jobs for recent college graduates will readily confirm, the reality is that there simply isn't much movement in salary available to these new college recruits. The entry-level hire generally does not have an employment track record on a professional level to provide any leverage for negotiation. Real negotiations on salary, benefits, retirement provisions, and so forth come to those with significant employment records at higher income levels.

Of course, the job offer is more than just money. It can be composed of geographic assignment, duties and responsibilities, training, benefits, health and medical insurance, educational assistance, car allowance or company vehicle, and a host of other items. All of this is generally detailed in the formal letter that presents the final job offer. In most cases this is a follow-up to a personal phone call from the employer representative who has been principally responsible for your hiring process.

That initial telephone offer is certainly binding as a verbal agreement, but most firms follow up with a detailed letter outlining the most significant parts of your employment contract. You may, of course, choose to respond immediately at the time of the telephone offer (which would be considered a binding oral contract), but you will also be required to formally answer the letter of offer with a letter of acceptance, restating the salient elements of the employer's description of your position, salary, and benefits. This ensures that both parties are clear on the terms and conditions of employment and remuneration and any other outstanding aspects of the job offer.

Is This the Job You Want?

Most new employees will respond affirmatively in writing, glad to be in the position to accept employment. If you've worked hard to get the offer and the job market is tight, other offers may not be in sight, so you will say, "Yes, I accept!" What is important here is that the job offer you accept be one that does fit your particular needs, values, and interests as you've outlined them in your self-assessment process. Moreover, it should be a job that will not only use your skills and education but also challenge you to develop new skills and talents.

Jobs are sometimes accepted too hastily, for the wrong reasons, and without proper scrutiny by the applicant. For example, an individual might readily accept a sales job only to find the continual rejection by potential clients unendurable. An office worker might realize within weeks the constraints of a desk job and yearn for more activity. Employment is an important part of our lives. It is, for most of our adult lives, our most continuous productive activity. We want to make good choices based on the right criteria.

If you have a low tolerance for risk, a job based on commission will certainly be very anxiety-provoking. If being near your family is important, issues of relocation could present a decision crisis for you. If you're an adventurous person, a job with frequent travel would provide needed excitement and be very desirable. The importance of income, the need to continue your education, your personal health situation—all of these have an impact on whether the job you are considering will ultimately meet your needs. Unless you've spent some time understanding and thinking about these issues, it will be difficult to evaluate offers you do receive.

More important, if you make a decision that you cannot tolerate and feel you must leave that job, you will then have both unemployment and self-esteem issues to contend with. These will combine to make the next job search tough going, indeed. So make your acceptance a carefully considered decision.

Negotiate Your Offer

It may be that there is some aspect of your job offer that is not particularly attractive to you. Perhaps there is no relocation allotment to help you move your possessions, and this presents some financial hardship for you. It may be that the health insurance is less than you had hoped. Your initial assignment may be different from what you expected, either in its location or in the duties and responsibilities that comprise it. Or it may simply be that the salary is less than you anticipated. Other considerations may be your official starting date of employment, vacation time, evening hours, dates of training programs or schools, and other concerns.

If you are considering not accepting the job because of some item or items in the job offer "package" that do not meet your needs, you should know that most employers emphatically wish that you would bring that issue to their attention. It may be that the employer can alter it to make the offer more agreeable for you. In some cases it cannot be changed. In any event the employer would generally like to have the opportunity to try to remedy a difficulty rather than risk losing a good potential employee over an issue that might have been resolved. After all, they have spent time and funds in securing your services, and they certainly deserve an opportunity to resolve any possible differences.

Honesty is the best approach in discussing any objections or uneasiness you might have over the employer's offer. Having received your formal offer in writing, contact your employer representative and indicate your particular dissatisfaction in a straightforward manner. For example, you might explain that while you are very interested in being employed by this organization, the salary (or any other benefit) is less than you have determined you require. State the terms you need, and listen to the response. You may be asked to put this in writing, or you may be asked to hold off until the firm can decide on a response. If you are dealing with a senior representative of the organization, one who has been involved in hiring for some time, you may get an immediate response or a solid indication of possible outcomes.

Perhaps the issue is one of relocation. Your initial assignment is in the Midwest, and because you had indicated a strong West Coast preference, you are surprised at the actual assignment. You might simply indicate that while you understand the need for the company to assign you based on its needs, you are disappointed and had hoped to be placed on the West Coast. You could inquire if that were still possible and, if not, would it be reasonable to expect a West Coast relocation in the future.

If your request is presented in a reasonable way, most employers will not see this as jeopardizing your offer. If they can agree to your proposal, they will. If not, they will simply tell you so, and you may choose to continue your candidacy with them or remove yourself from consideration. The choice will be up to you.

Some firms will adjust benefits within their parameters to meet the candidate's need if at all possible. If a candidate requires a relocation cost allowance, he or she may be asked to forgo tuition benefits for the first year to accomplish this adjustment. An increase in life insurance may be adjusted by some other benefit trade-off; perhaps a family dental plan is not needed. In these decisions you are called upon, sometimes under time pressure, to know how you value these issues and how important each is to you.

Many employers find they are more comfortable negotiating for candidates who have unique qualifications or who bring especially needed expertise to the organization. Employers hiring large numbers of entry-level college graduates may be far more reluctant to accommodate any changes in offer conditions. They are well supplied with candidates with similar education and experience so that if rejected by one candidate, they can draw new candidates from an ample labor pool.

Compare Offers

The condition of the economy, the job seeker's academic major and particular geographic job market, and individual needs and demands for certain employment conditions may not provide more than one job offer at a time. Some job seekers may feel that no reasonable offer should go unaccepted for the simple fear there won't be another.

In a tough job market, or if the job you seek is not widely available, or when your job search goes on too long and becomes difficult to sustain financially and emotionally, it may be necessary to accept an inferior offer. The alternative is continued unemployment. Even here, when you feel you don't have a choice, you can at least understand that in accepting this particular offer, there may be limitations and conditions you don't appreciate. At the time of acceptance, there were no other alternatives, but you can begin to use that position to gain the experience and talent to move toward a more attractive position.

Sometimes, however, more than one offer is received, and the candidate has the luxury of choice. If the job seeker knows what he or she wants and has done the necessary self-assessment honestly and thoroughly, it may be clear that one of the offers conforms more closely to those expressed wants and needs.

However, if, as so often happens, the offers are similar in terms of conditions and salary, the question then becomes which organization might provide the necessary climate, opportunities, and advantages for your professional development and growth. This is the time when solid employer research and astute questioning during the interviews really pay off. How much did you learn about the employer through your own research and skillful questioning? When the interviewer asked during the interview "Do you have any questions?" did you ask the kinds of questions that would help resolve a choice between one organization and another? Just as an employer must decide among numerous applicants, so must the applicant learn to assess the potential employer. Both are partners in the job search.

Reneging on an Offer

An especially disturbing occurrence for employers and career counseling professionals is when a job seeker formally (either orally or by written contract) accepts employment with one organization and later reneges on the agreement and goes with another employer.

There are all kinds of rationalizations offered for this unethical behavior. None of them satisfies. The sad irony is that what the job seeker is willing to do to the employer—make a promise and then break it—he or she would be outraged to have done to him- or herself: have the job offer pulled. It is a very bad way to begin a career. It suggests the individual has not taken the time to do the necessary self-assessment and self-awareness exercises to think and judge critically. The new offer taken may, in fact, be no better or worse than the one refused. You should be aware that there have been incidents of legal action following job candidates' reneging on an offer. This adds a very sour note to what should be a harmonious beginning of a lifelong adventure.

PART TWO

THE CAREER PATHS

5

Introduction to the Engineering Career Paths

Over the course of your career, your professional development will continue to involve personal growth as you adjust to a wide variety of experiences. Your career development as an engineer will depend on your ability to stay up to date on the new technologies and skill sets required in the rapidly changing workplace. You will have opportunities to do this through further formal education as well as distance learning and employer-provided training.

Thoughtful consideration of the knowledge and skills that your field demands and your own interests, values, and goals, as described in Part One, is essential but it will not be enough. You must also consider the needs, goals, values, and culture of the organizations in which you consider working. Is there a good "fit" between you and these organizations? Many times you will not be sure, but an assessment can result in new and exciting opportunities that you might not have ever considered.

Because you have chosen a field that has demanded a lot of you academically and personally, you can now follow many avenues to enhance your personal and professional growth. However, keep in mind that your employer is only responsible for your growth and development to the extent that it benefits the organizational goals. Ultimately, you are responsible for your own professional growth and development. This does not mean that your goals can supersede those of the organization for which you work. It means that you have a responsibility to find an employer, or opportunities within a workplace, where the goals, values, and culture are compatible with your style of working, interacting, and learning.

Part Two of this book presents various career paths available to engineers. Each represents a different way in which you can attain your personal career goal. The characteristics and demands of each path will help you identify options that appear to be a best fit for you. With more research and exploration, you will have a better basis for identifying the path that is best for you. Your most desirable path can help form the basis for your career plan, and a career plan will give your personal goals credibility and your job search focus.

If you are just beginning your career in engineering as a freshman or sophomore, explore one or two of these career paths more in depth during your undergraduate experience. Reading about them will not be enough. Talking to professional engineers will be helpful, but a word of caution. Input of this nature is subjective, not fact. To really evaluate whether the information you have gathered is correct for you, get out in the field and try out your initial decisions through faculty research, summer internships, and/or alternating cooperative education (co-op) experience. The process of experiencing the nature of the work will help you find your niche. In addition, this experience will be highly valued when you begin applying for your first permanent position or seeking admission to graduate school.

In the field of engineering, there are many opportunities to do these things. Involvement in faculty research, for example, is an excellent way to evaluate an academic career path. Summer jobs and internships can be helpful too. While industry typically thinks of internships for students between their junior and senior year, those students who will graduate in the following academic year, there are usually many opportunities for summer jobs that will provide a brief but valuable exposure to an industry or an area in your engineering discipline where you feel you may have an interest.

In addition, you should be aware that co-op is a very well-known, and widely respected, means of assimilation into the field of engineering. Since 1906, co-op has been the means by which hundreds of thousands of engineers have tested their initial decision in the real world and gone on to pursue rewarding careers in business, industry, government, and academia. Unlike humanities internships—which consist of one term on a special project—traditional co-op students alternate periods of paid employment in engineering with periods of academic study. They usually return to the same co-op employer over time. This process allows them to become part of the mainstream of an engineering team in their organization well before graduation. They not only further develop their technical skills but also enhance their sense of professional judgment and awareness about aspects of their field that they like or dislike.

Co-op is not unlike taking a college course while in high school. That experience provides high school students with a chance to "see what it's like" in college before they actually get there. Co-op does the same thing for undergraduate engineering students. It provides an opportunity to "see what it's like" in business, industry, or government. You may find your niche in one of these areas or learn early in your career experience that this is not the best fit for you. Learning that during your undergraduate experience and having time to alter your goals and direction is much better than coming to this realization after investing four years in undergraduate study and several years in a job you find that you do not enjoy!

About Your Grades and Your Engineering Career

People might tell you that once you are in the field of engineering it is not the institution you attended or the grades you got in school that will make the difference, it is what you do on the job that counts. This advice might be true in some organizations, but there is one significant catch!

You must land that first job before you get the opportunity to prove what you can do. In today's work environment, most employers, from sports teams to industry, are not willing to take chances on unproven ability. Your academic performance is seen as a significant measure of how seriously you have approached your college career and your major.

If you have attained a high grade point average, you are to be congratulated! Engineering is not an easy major and your accomplishments are not to be minimized. However, you need to be aware that high grades may help you obtain an interview but they do not guarantee job offers.

Employers who seek candidates with high grade point averages have, in effect, leveled the playing field. In other words, if all candidates for an entry-level engineering position must have a high grade point average, the candidates have to set themselves apart in areas such as activities, skills, experiences, honors, and so forth. Your grade point average, in these instances, might get you the interview, but it is all of the other qualities, characteristics, and skills that you bring to the organization that will get you the offer.

Conversely, if your grades are not what you wish them to be, you cannot let that paralyze you in terms of your job search. It does not matter if the search is for a co-op position, an internship, or a permanent position. Cover letters, interviewing, and letters of recommendation sometimes can be used to provide a credible explanation for your grade situation. An example may be a decision to attend a more difficult university or to take an honors or graduate-level course. This decision demonstrates that you are not afraid of a challenge and also says that you have a higher level of knowledge than you would had you stayed at a more comfortable level for you.

In other cases, it will be important for you to be flexible and to set your sights on organizations and experiences that can build your skill set and provide you with an opportunity to establish your professional reputation as an engineer. In most cases, you will probably not be at a Fortune 500 company initially, but it does not mean you are never going to get there if that is your goal.

The best course of action, however, is to work to correct the grade point average dilemma. This is particularly true if you have a few more terms of study. If you are in your freshman or sophomore year, develop a specific plan to correct the problems that you see that you are having. If you are a junior, concentrate on your major courses and set a goal of increasing your grade point average in the major. There may be nothing that you can do about that grade in freshman calculus, but you can work to have strong grades in your systems physiology classes, if you are a biomedical engineering major.

Summary

As you explore the various career paths in engineering, you will come to appreciate the variety and the challenge that awaits you. Try not to let the options overwhelm and frustrate you. At this stage of your career, you are learning to make career decisions. Nothing is irreversible, and all hold great opportunity for personal and professional growth.

You actually know more about yourself than you realize. You have close to twenty years or more of experience being you! While you have to watch out for stereotypes about jobs, occupations, and organizations, don't ignore your intuitive reactions to your experiences in engineering. Those reactions are based on your personal preferences and strengths and should not be ignored as you begin to make decisions.

You have a diverse group of people, including trusted faculty members, work supervisors, and family members, as "sounding boards" to listen, react, and help you process the information you will be assembling. This is an invaluable tool in your career planning and job search. However, it is important to remember that you ultimately will make the decisions, and you will want to make decisions that keep as many opportunities open to you as possible. This provides flexibility for the future and ensures that you maintain maximum control over your own career development.

6

Path I:
Industry

Industry has always provided engineers with an abundant and diverse range of career paths leading to personal and professional growth. However, in recent years, the employment landscape has changed dramatically because of the globalization of the workplace and the automation/computerization of many processes. Nonetheless, industry remains a significant employer of entry-level engineers.

New engineers should be aware that, because of rapidly changing business demands, careers in industry will not follow the traditional paths of the past and that obtaining positions in industry will be increasingly competitive. Several factors are contributing to this new reality:

1. Manufacturing is no longer old, dirty "smokestacks."
2. Today's industry is influenced by globalization.
3. Organizations have more flattened advancement structures.
4. An increasing number of small and midsize companies serve major corporations.

First, today's manufacturers are no longer dirty "smokestack" industries. Modern manufacturing facilities are highly automated, with many relying on robots to perform tasks formerly done by factory workers. It is now the responsibility of a few highly trained engineers to manage the production process and keep the robotic equipment at peak performance levels. In fact, many manufacturing facilities have taken on the appearance of high-tech centers instead of the stereotypical twentieth-century factory. As a result of this modernization, manufacturing facilities now require cross-disciplinary teams and creative problem solving that only highly educated engineers can provide. The new manufacturing environment requires high levels of engineering expertise combined with the ability to work with and lead diverse groups of people (employees, suppliers, consultants) in different locations to meet a common goal. Today's engineers must have communication skills that are as strong as their engineering skills.

Second, today's industry is strongly influenced by globalization. In addition to seeking new markets for products around the world, business and industry seek global suppliers of raw goods and remote manufacturers of products in order to keep costs down and profits high for their shareholders. With global competition expected to expand, companies are seeking versatility in their workforce. This means that industry will draw from a global pool of talent, making the job market very competitive for engineers who do not have the skills required to function in a global environment. While high-level engineering skills will always be necessary, today's job candidates will need to demonstrate strong oral and written communication skills as well. Cultural awareness, the ability to work well in a diverse environment, and even foreign language skills will be much sought after. Engineers who possess both high-level technical skills and these "softer" skills will be in high demand.

According to Steve Jahnke of Texas Instruments, some of the major challenges that companies face today are knowing what products to design for international markets and how to work with international engineering teams (be they in India, China, or elsewhere). The ability to work with both U.S. and offshore engineering and marketing teams is, and will be, highly valued by industry. Engineers with this type of experience and ability can put things in context for both management teams in ways that are more clearly understood. Steve sees this as one of the benefits of the "free trade and offshoring" debate. He suggests that ten years ago, he might not have been as highly valued as he is now. His years of experience living and working in another country, and his strong engineering knowledge have resulted in promotions and compensation comparable to that for MBA consultants/finance specialists.

A third reality affecting industry is flattened organizational structures. Most industries have eliminated the hierarchical levels of advancement that engineers came to expect.

That structure has been replaced with an emphasis on teamwork and projects. Contributions of engineering and cross-functional teams now give companies their competitive edge. The new platform for career advancement is your ability to make significant contributions in different business functions and to a wide variety of teams and projects, which increase in scope of work and financial value to the company.

The new rules for success include, but are not limited to:

- Continually expanding and enhancing your engineering knowledge to keep your company aware of emerging technologies that will help it to be more competitive
- Broadening your knowledge of your company's products, processes, and facilities to be ready to contribute when there is a business need
- Managing diverse groups of people as well as being able to influence and persuade others throughout the organization, even if they do not directly report to you

Many industry leaders recommend that engineers manage their own career development by acquiring a broad knowledge of company products, processes, services, and locations. In addition, they recommend being capable of "deep dives" into one or more technical areas. In other words, management expects engineers who advance within the organization to not only be Subject Matter Experts (SME) in a particular aspect of engineering but also to have extensive knowledge of the company's products, processes, and services and be able to lead many different groups of people in achieving business goals.

The fourth factor impacting a change in engineers' career development is the emergence of small and midsize companies that serve as designers, suppliers, manufacturers, and/or distributors for major industries. Because these companies tend to lack the bureaucratic restrictions of larger organizations, they are able to respond more quickly to changing demands in the marketplace. Consequently, they provide new challenges and new levels of responsibility for creative and energetic engineers, and opportunities for rapid advancement within the organization, the industry, and the profession.

This means that new engineers have to be more versatile and sensitive to the changing needs and expectations of industry. They also have to think about their careers in different ways than the engineers who have gone before them. As in the past, creativity, problem solving, and technical expertise are important. However, in today's engineering job market, they might not be enough. Engineers will need to demonstrate knowledge of leading software applications in their field, strong teamwork skills, leadership potential, multicultural awareness, and an entrepreneurial spirit. Because the engineering profession is changing rapidly, it offers new and exciting opportunities for engineers who are eager to contribute and solve problems.

Definition of the Career Path

Because of the nature of your engineering education, you should not be surprised to find that in ten to fifteen years after leaving school, your career direction may be very far from your original area of expertise. This is not cause for alarm but a validation of the strength and flexibility of your engineering degree and the great career variety that is available when you elect the industrial career path.

When you consider that only one-third of the courses that you take as an undergraduate are unique to your specialization, it is not surprising that you will have a high degree of flexibility in pursuing your engineering career. Because the balance of your course work encompasses other engineering disciplines as well as mathematics, science, and liberal arts, you have the foundation for several career scenarios in business and industry.

The diversity of opportunity also brings a challenge. The many job titles that you will find in the field of engineering might be overwhelming at first. A quick glance at the engineering section of job websites or publications will reveal a wide variety of job titles, everything from applications engineer to xerography engineer! As you read the ads, you will see that some applications engineers require a B.S. in mechanical engineering, while others require a B.S. in electrical engineering or maybe computer engineering. All of this reflects the variety that awaits you.

Now is the time to begin regularly reading trade publications in your discipline, including the classified sections in the back. This will help you become familiar with the job titles and the responsibilities of people in your field and with specific industry advances. You should also read a general engineering trade publication so that you stay abreast of developments in fields that complement your own. As you gain more experience, both on-the-job and through continuing education, this practice will help you see emerging trends and how to prepare for them.

Some Career Choices in Engineering

According to Peterson's *Job Opportunities for Engineering, Science, and Computer Graduates*, there are seven functional areas in which engineers tend to work: accounting and finance; administration; information systems processing; marketing and sales; production/operations; research and development;

and technical/professional services. These functional areas can be further categorized into two groupings: those functions that require the direct application of one's engineering expertise and those functions that do not, in and of themselves, have an engineering emphasis but require an engineering background. These tracks are often referred to as the *technical track* versus the *management track*.

To advance within an organization, it is important to learn about the professional and educational experiences of its senior management. This information will help you evaluate whether this is a company where you can build the kind of career you envision. Do not be surprised to find that the careers of senior management were NOT straight paths to the top. Most of today's senior managers and executives have advanced their careers through a wide variety of positions within various companies, business units, and engineering functions.

If your goal is to someday be part of an executive team, you need to study the promotion practices of the industries and companies in which you are interested. If you want to go as far as you can in a manner that best fits you, it is important to know which businesses and industries provide what you are seeking.

The Functional Areas on the Technical Track

Engineers who want to develop their engineering expertise tend to elect the "technical track" as their career path. In the functional areas associated with this track, engineers can acquire advanced knowledge in the engineering, scientific, and technical aspects of their discipline.

Research and Development (R&D). Research engineers are engaged in systematic and critical investigations leading to the acquisition of knowledge for a specific application. As a separate component, development engineers design, construct, and test prototypes and models, including setting up and operating pilot plants (small-scale operations that are tested before large-scale production facilities are built). In this area, product development and process development refer to the development of new or improved products or manufacturing processes.

Previously, research engineers in industry and academia were engaged in investigation that might or might not be for a specific purpose. However, the global market has put increased emphasis on solving specific problems or developing new product lines in order to remain competitive and to sustain future corporate growth. To this end, some corporations continue to support centralized R&D and/or R&D units within major operating facilities, but in recent years R&D has seen dramatic cuts in many organizations. Some companies have cut their own research expenditures but have developed partnerships with government laboratories and university faculty and municipal research parks in order to maintain a competitive edge.

Microsoft is a notable exception. In an interview on CNN, Bill Gates talked about corporate research and its role at Microsoft. According to Gates, "research is the lifeblood of innovation in the economy." However, even the recognized leaders in corporate research, Xerox and AT&T, have challenges translating their research into profitable products. Microsoft Research made a commitment not only to have great researchers, but also to get from research to usable products.

Every year, Microsoft holds Tech Fest, a company festival where Microsoft engineers and computer scientists get to see and discuss all of Microsoft's research advances. As a result, some very innovative technologies have been included in products such as operating systems and Xbox. For example, the depiction of grass and trees in Xbox are very realistic. That's the result of a technique developed by one of Microsoft's researchers.

Production. Engineers in production are central to the mission of the business or industry. This is the area in which ideas are taken from the design stage to finished, marketable products. The production engineers are involved in every phase of producing the product, from specifying materials to designing the work flow. The production area is responsible for all tasks necessary to produce a product or system on time and within budget. This generally includes scheduling materials and personnel as well as specifying machine usage, materials-handling procedures, and/or control methods. It often includes personnel training and supervision.

With increased globalization of product manufacturing, production engineers are more frequently sent to overseas facilities to monitor and guide corporate production specifications. This means working with diverse teams of people to improve efficiency or accomplish a production goal.

While manufacturing engineering is often associated with making a product, construction engineering and mining engineering may also be included in this category. The processes and the skills necessary for producing a building or extracting raw materials from the earth are very similar to what happens in a manufacturing environment.

Technical/Professional Services. Technical services include a wide range of functions in support of the business or industry. These functions can range from design and testing to feasibility studies and consulting. Engineers in this area assume responsibility for short-term or long-term projects that need resolution so that the product, process, or system can be improved. For example, a recent hire at International Paper provides technical support to various converting facilities around the country. As a mechanical engineer, his responsibilities include troubleshooting machinery that is not performing properly and analyzing production operations to identify areas that need improvement.

While project engineer is the most visible job title in this functional area, technical services include a wide range of occupation specialties such as chemical engineer, materials engineer, and biomedical engineer. There are also engineering positions named according to the technology with which they are associated, such as the control systems engineer and the environmental engineer.

Positions in this functional area exist at both corporate and plant levels and provide excellent opportunities for new engineers. New engineers might think it best to start in the corporate office, but the majority of fast-track engineers, those who move up the career ladder the fastest, start at the plant level. One reason that plant-level experience is preferred is that these positions provide an excellent way to learn about all aspects of the product, the company, and its customers and competition. Success at the plant level can lead to senior engineering positions and management positions at plant and corporate levels.

As with the production area in industry, the technical services area in service industries is often considered a "line" function. However, technical services are not limited to industry career paths. You will find technical services opportunities in the consulting, government, and academic career paths as well.

The Functional Areas on the Management Track

While you will need to have experiences in some of the technical/engineering areas of the industry or company, engineers in the management track gain experience in the business side as well. These areas typically include:

- **Marketing and sales.** Although there are certainly exceptions as a result of the breadth of academic preparation that engineers have, most engineers involved in this functional area work for businesses and industries that produce technical products or services. Sometimes their work is actually referred to as "technology marketing." In many companies this is one of the better paths to corporate management for engineers, as it not only requires technical expertise but it provides a broad overview of the customer base, research and development, production, distribution, and product reliability. While some organizations hire entry-level engineers in technical sales, this functional area generally seeks experienced engineers.

• **Information systems processing.** Engineers in this functional area are concerned with software applications, not computer equipment. This area of business and industry is of paramount importance because the leading software applications, such as SAP, not only manage administrative functions but also production controls and distribution. Those engineers involved in this area analyze, design, develop, and implement these types of systems as the backbone of the company or organization. Because of the diversity of opportunity and application, engineers in this area can concentrate on business systems applications, scientific applications, or other analytical specialties such as mathematical or statistical modeling.

• **Accounting and finance.** While all types of engineers are involved in this area, industrial engineers seem to be most in demand because of their quantitative skills. In this functional area, engineers become involved in financial analysis, operations research, strategic planning, and actuarial work. The settings in which these engineers are employed range from hospitals to manufacturing companies. Banks and insurance companies increasingly recruit engineers for this area.

• **Administration.** In this area, engineers are involved in the nontechnical aspects of business and industry. This may include government compliance or community relations. Nonetheless, the technical expertise of engineers in this area is a basic requirement. In large organizations, the administrative functions have traditionally been performed from the corporate headquarters. While this is still true in some companies, increasingly these functions are being performed closer to the technical operations because of corporate downsizing, increased reliance on outside suppliers, and the proliferation of midsize and small businesses and industries. This is more likely to be an area into which an engineer is moved or promoted, rather than an area in which an entry-level engineer begins.

Beyond the Functional Areas

To provide a broad overview of the functions and career possibilities in the various functional areas within an organization, many large employers now hire engineers into rotational developmental programs after college. These programs can be called Engineering Development Programs (EDPs), Management Development Programs (MDPs), or Leadership Development Programs (LDPs). When hired into one of these programs, you can expect to hold four- to twelve-month rotational assignments, over two or more years, through some of the functional areas mentioned above.

These programs offer an excellent opportunity to gain a good overview of the organization. At the same time it provides the organization the opportunity to assess you for possible higher-level positions within the organization during the course of your career.

Some of these programs work in tandem with selected business schools. When the time is right the employer will have successful graduates of the developmental program apply to these schools for admission on a part-time or full-time basis. In many cases, the employer pays these costs in return for your remaining with the organization for a specified number of years.

If the developmental program does not have an associated business school and you want to attend business school after working several years, it is important to know that most top business schools will not count the years that you spent rotating to different functional areas. You will still need to have three or more years of experience beyond the rotational program. Business schools want to see your impact within an organization. Therefore, if you are eager to go on to business school as soon as possible you might want to consider "line" positions in a specific functional area, particularly one of the technical functional areas that are highly valued by business schools.

How Engineering Careers Progress in Industry

The U.S. Department of Labor Statistics identified eight different engineering levels that described the progression of responsibility for engineers. As industry flattened organizational structures, the eight engineering levels have become five. However, that doesn't mean faster advancement. In fact, progress from one level to another takes longer because the scope of responsibilities and corporate expectations of the original eight levels of engineering are still expected for advancement today. The following list shows how Hoover's Online describes the five levels of engineering for mechanical engineers:

• **Level I mechanical engineer.** Designs, develops, and tests all aspects of mechanical components, equipment, and machinery. Applies knowledge of engineering principles to design products such as engines, instruments, controls, robots, machines, etc. May be involved in fabrication, operation, application, installation, and/or repair of mechanical products. May require a bachelor's degree in engineering and zero to three years of experience in the field or in a related area. Has knowledge of commonly used concepts, practices, and procedures within a particular field. Relies on instructions and preestablished guidelines to perform the functions of the job. Works under immediate supervision. Primary job functions do not typically require exercising independent judgment. Typically reports to a supervisor or manager. Alternate job title: entry-level mechanical engineer.

- **Level II mechanical engineer.** Designs, develops, and tests all aspects of mechanical components, equipment, and machinery. Applies knowledge of engineering principles to design products such as engines, instruments, controls, robots, machines, etc. May be involved in fabrication, operation, application, installation, and/or repair of mechanical products. Requires a bachelor's degree in engineering and two to five years of experience in the field or in a related area. Familiar with standard concepts, practices, and procedures within a particular field. Relies on limited experience and judgment to plan and accomplish goals. Performs a variety of tasks. Works under general supervision; typically reports to a supervisor or manager. A certain degree of creativity and latitude is required. Alternate job title: intermediate-level mechanical engineer.

- **Level III mechanical engineer.** Designs, develops, and tests all aspects of mechanical components, equipment, and machinery. Applies knowledge of engineering principles to design products such as engines, instruments, controls, robots, machines, etc. May be involved in fabrication, operation, application, installation, and/or repair of mechanical products. Requires a bachelor's degree in engineering and four to six years of experience in the field or in a related area. Familiar with a variety of the field's concepts, practices, and procedures. Relies on experience and judgment to plan and accomplish goals. Performs a variety of complicated tasks. May report to an executive or a manager. A wide degree of creativity and latitude is expected.

- **Level IV mechanical engineer.** Designs, develops, and tests all aspects of mechanical components, equipment, and machinery. Applies knowledge of engineering principles to design products such as engines, instruments, controls, robots, machines, etc. May be involved in fabrication, operation, application, installation, and/or repair of mechanical products. Requires a bachelor's degree in engineering and five to eight years of experience in the field or in a related area. Familiar with a variety of the field's concepts, practices, and procedures. Relies on extensive experience and judgment to plan and accomplish goals. Performs a variety of tasks. May lead and direct the work of others. A wide degree of creativity and latitude is expected. Typically reports to a manager or head of a unit/department. Alternate job title: mechanical engineer—project lead.

- **Level V mechanical engineer.** Designs, develops, and tests all aspects of mechanical components, equipment, and machinery. Applies knowledge of engineering principles to design products such as engines, instruments, controls, robots, machines, etc. May be involved in fabrication, operation, application, installation, and/or repair of mechanical products. Requires a bachelor's degree in engineering and at least eight years of experience in the field or in a related area. Familiar with a variety of the field's concepts, practices, and procedures. Relies on extensive experience and judgment to plan and accomplish goals. Performs a variety of tasks. May lead and direct the work of others. A wide degree of creativity and latitude is expected. Typically reports to a manager or head of a unit/department. Alternate job titles: mechanical engineer-consultant/mechanical engineer-specialist.

Source: Hoover's Online, http://swz-hoovers.salary.com, May 2007

Working Conditions

Unlike many other professions, which often have a limited range of work settings and conditions, engineers are virtually everywhere! The versatility of the discipline and the analytical and problem-solving skills of individual engineers make them sought after by both service and manufacturing industries. Some of the types of industries in which engineers work include:

Computer hardware/software
Data communications/processing
Design and development
Distribution
Energy
Entertainment
Financial services
Manufacturing
Medical and pharmaceutical
Oil and gas
Telecommunications
Diversified companies

Employment options within these areas can be broken down more specifically to types of products and services. Some of these include:

Abrasive and polishing products
Agricultural services and equipment
Aircraft and aerospace

Air transportation
Ammunition and related products
Amusement and recreation
Automobile manufacturing and services
Bakery products
Balances and scales
Boilermaking
Brick, tile, and nonclay refractory
Building materials
Business services
Chemical
Concrete products
Construction
Coating
Electronics
Electroplating
Explosives
Fabricated metals and plastics
Financial
Food products
Foundry
Furniture and household products
Garment
Glass manufacturing
Hardware
Heat treatment
Instruments and apparatus
Iron and steel
Laundry
Leather manufacturing
Lighting fixtures
Machinery manufacturing
Manufactured buildings
Medical services and health care
Mining
Motion picture
Nonferrous metal alloys
Optical goods
Paint and varnish

Paper and pulp
Petroleum
Photographic apparatus and materials
Pipeline operation
Plastic materials
Polymer
Pottery and porcelain
Printing and publishing
Refrigerator and refrigeration
Railroad transportation
Rubber
Sanitary
Sporting goods
Structural and ornamental metalwork
Telecommunication
Textile
Tobacco
Transportation
Welding and related processes
Wood distillation

Corporate Technology Information Services, Inc. (CorpTech) publishes a directory of U.S. high-technology company profiles. It uses seventeen unique industry codes to group these industries, and secondary classifications that define their products or services. The CorpTech industry list includes:

Factory automation
Biotechnology
Chemicals
Computer hardware
Defense
Energy
Environmental
Manufacturing equipment
Advanced materials
Medical
Pharmaceuticals
Photonics
Computer software

Subassemblies and components
Test and measurement
Telecommunications
Internet transportation

If you are not sure what you want to do with your engineering degree, it's likely that you do have some ideas about the type of industry, setting, or products/services that interests you. Your preferred geographic location might help narrow the field. For example, if you are a chemical engineer who prefers to live in the Midwest, opportunities in the oil and petroleum industries might not be as numerous as they would be if you lived in the Gulf Coast region of the country. However, opportunities with companies in the agricultural industry will be higher. Nonetheless, engineering employment possibilities are everywhere. That provides great flexibility for managing your career development.

Education and Qualifications

A bachelor's degree in engineering provides you with a wide range of career options, because an accredited engineering program requires two years of math, physics, chemistry, and introductory engineering courses as well as two years of course work in your major. In addition, you can specialize within your major. Engineering concentrations further qualify you for specific engineering positions and/or specific industries. For example, a biomedical engineer might elect a specialization in biomechanics or in signal processing, while a mechanical engineer might specialize in micro-electro-mechanical systems machinery (MEMs) or robotics or nanotechnology.

The foreign language, humanities, social sciences, and English courses that you take, in addition to the rigorous background of math, science, and engineering, greatly strengthen your qualifications for a variety of engineering positions in a global economy. Engineering graduates sometimes decide to pursue graduate and professional degrees either before entering industry or after they have been working for several years. While some obtain master's and doctoral degrees in engineering, others pursue graduate and professional degrees in business or public administration, law, or medicine to advance their careers within industry.

Advanced degrees offer additional opportunities in the industry career path, particularly when they are combined with hands-on experience. You should investigate the industry you plan to enter to determine if there is a salary differential if you were to obtain a master's or doctoral degree before accepting a position. In some companies, work experience is so valued that a master's degree without industry experience does not result in a significant salary difference when compared to bachelor's-level hires with at least one year of co-op experience or one year of full-time work experience.

Timing and finances are serious considerations when making the decision to pursue graduate or professional education. The more education you have, the more doors are open to you over the course of your career. This is increasingly true for Ph.D. level engineers with industry experience. Industry, consulting, and academia all seek these individuals. However, pursuing graduate study without a personal focus on the specialization you want to study and why you are pursuing the degree can be frustrating. This is another career decision that should be reached using the self-assessment strategies discussed in Part One of this book.

Earnings

In both boom times and downturns, engineering graduates are able to command top dollar for their skills, according to the National Association of Colleges and Employers (NACE). Even during economic downturns, when engineering graduates experience challenges in obtaining job offers, NACE reports that engineering and computer science graduates still receive "substantial starting salary offers."

The 2006 NACE Salary Survey reported that engineering graduates in:

Mechanical engineering had an average starting salary offer of $54,587.
Chemical engineering had an average starting salary offer of $60,054.
Civil engineering had an average starting salary offer of $47,145.
Electrical engineering had an average starting salary offer of $54,599.

Starting salaries change year to year and region to region. It is advisable to use a variety of salary databases to stay up to date on engineering salaries. A few online options are

Engineering Salary Calculator (engineersalary.com)
Engineering Central (http://engineeringcentral.salary.com)
Hoover's Online (http://swz-hoovers.salary.com)

By using these databases, it is possible to obtain salary information on a wide range of entry-level engineering positions by geographic area. In addition, most of the sites provide descriptions of entry-level engineering positions in industry. It is important to note that if you have less continuous, full-time experience than listed in some of the descriptions, you can expect salary offers to be lower. If you believe that your background might qualify you for a higher level of compensation than you are offered, you might consider negotiating for an earlier review with the possibility of a pay increase.

Salary information changes quickly. Many factors impact the rate of pay offered to entry-level engineers. Some of those factors include, but are not limited to, national and international economic conditions and specific conditions in the industry and/or company that you may be considering. Therefore, it is advisable to read the business section of major newspapers or their online editions; read trade journals in your areas of interest; study job postings online and on company websites; and use salary websites listed in this book to check current salary information yourself.

Career Outlook

The continued demand for new and improved products, the increasing number of technological advances that impact our daily lives, and the growing need for more economical manufacturing and systems processes to remain competitive in a global market indicate that there is an exciting and dynamic future for engineers who pursue an industry career path. There are always exciting new possibilities in the field of engineering. Some of the emerging technologies include: advanced materials, advanced semiconductor devices, artificial intelligence, biotechnology, business intelligence, digital imaging technology, flexible computer-integrated manufacturing, high-density data storage, high-performance computing, Internet technology, medical devices and diagnostics, nanotechnology, optoelectronics, sensor technology, and superconductors. As you plan for the future, you may want to consider some of these emerging technologies when selecting your area of specialization within your engineering discipline.

A special note: It is not necessary for engineers to begin their career in industry to have a successful career path in the private sector. For example, engineers who initially join federal or state regulatory agencies and gain several years of experience find it easy to move into industrial positions. Increasingly, industry places a high premium on both engineering knowledge and a strong understanding of government regulations. For example, the vice president of government relations for a major manufacturer of household appliances has stated that the appliance industry's greatest challenge comes primarily from governments. The industry is increasingly involved in reengineering products to meet national and international regulations. To remain competitive, more and more companies rely on engineers to keep pace not only with technological advances, but also with government regulation, which can have the tendency to push technical feasibility further and further. It becomes the engineer's job to manage these regulations with a sensitivity to cost, performance, manufacturability, and reliability.

This is particularly true in the health-care industry, which is heavily regulated by both the Food and Drug Administration and the Environmental Protection Agency. Likewise, companies seeking to do business in foreign markets seek engineers who are familiar with international standards, such as ISO 9000, the quality-management system in production environments or ISO 10006 the quality management guidelines for project management.

To remain competitive, industry must rely on research and development. Research efforts develop new technologies for the marketplace. Develop efforts result in addressing the applications of new technologies to the challenges that face manufacturing, suppliers, vendors, and/or customers. While much research and development occurs in academia and the government career paths, those industries that remain in the forefront of their field always invest a percentage of their profits in research and development, also referred to as R&D. Typical investment of profits ranges from 5 to 15 percent, depending on the industry. Industries that invest in R&D include:

R&D as % of Sales

Aerospace	4.6
Chemicals	4.1
Health	7.2
IT Hardware	9.5
Computer Software	10.3
Pharma & Biotech	15.1

A sample of the job descriptions that one might find in the area of R&D is:

Junior R&D Project Engineer. B.S. or master's degree in an engineering discipline with strong background in physical sciences. Exceptional performance in course work and extensive experience in independent completion of design projects incorporating optical and analytical elements.

Required skills: familiarity with optical systems, laser design, and test methods; knowledge of laser material processing or laser/tissue interaction; optical specification (polymer, glass, coatings, crystals, UV, and NIR materials); ability to model/program in LabView, MathCad, or MatLab, and in Excel; optical sensor design and testing; data analysis and reporting, presenting results to colleagues, project documentation; exceptional interpersonal skills for a fast-paced laboratory environment

Product Development Engineer. Ph.D. in materials science, chemical engineering, or mechanical engineering preferred. Candidate must demonstrate thorough capability of conducting research and development in the area of materials science, tribology, friction phenomena, transport phenomena, friction and related systems, and computer modeling and of using analytical tools and facilities necessary for the research, development, and analysis of new transmission systems friction products. Prior experience in friction materials development for "wet" clutch, dry brakes, or friction-related applications. Required skills are research experience in computer modeling, research experience in friction test methods and test equipment, familiarity with analytical methods and computational methods, strong communication skills, self starter, demonstrated potential for project management, demonstrated abilities in both research and development

Strategy for Finding the Jobs

The following are tips for conducting a job search in engineering:

Set specific goals.
Keep a "to-do" list.
Maintain a calendar to record information and meetings.
Tailor your résumé and cover letter to specific types of positions.
Target specific companies that are of interest to you.
Develop your networking skills.
Broaden your network with each contact.
Prepare well for each interview.

Research each company.

Know the company's operations, products, and current market situation.

Know why you want to work for that company.

Know how to describe your background in twenty seconds.

Be able to clearly articulate your skills, interests, and abilities.

Know what you want to convey about yourself and make sure that you do.

Master the art of the "Behavioral Interview," also known in the engineering field as "Competency Based Interviewing."

There are numerous online sites that can help you prepare:

brockport.edu/career/behave.htm

uwec.edu/Career/online_library/behavioral_int.htm

umt.edu/career/interviewing/behavior.htm

careerjournal.com/jobhunting/interviewing/19980129-vogt.html

After conducting the self-awareness process outlined in Part One of this book, the next step, and the very best strategy for finding an engineering job in industry, is research, research, research!

Search engines are one of your best friends when it comes to researching companies, but a word of caution before you begin. Most job openings are not posted on the Internet, so to make sure that you are tapping into the best available jobs in your field, work with your career services office, network through the many contacts you have off and on campus, and read trade journals in your engineering field. All of these strategies are important for a successful job search.

It's also important to remember that there is a great deal of glossy corporate literature and Internet information for some companies. As a result, there might be a tendency to develop myths about the working conditions of organizations portrayed in such a fashion. You need to go beyond corporate recruiting literature and really get to know the organization before you accept a job. While you will want to do much of this research before applying and interviewing for a job, it is good to remember that the interview, particularly site interviews, will be an important element of your research before accepting a job offer.

Resources for Your Job Search

If you have completed your self-assessment and are ready to begin your search for an engineering position in industry, there are numerous resources available to you. They range from your campus career services office to the Internet. The most important thing to remember is that the research you conduct on companies and the knowledge that you have about their product, their competition, their goals, and their structure will not only help you determine if a particular organization is the "best fit" for you, but it will also set you apart in the interviews. In addition, this knowledge of the employer will give you a real advantage if you decide to accept an offer and begin your career with the organization. To help you get started, the following career and job websites have been identified by engineering discipline:

Acoustical Engineering
http://asa.aip.org/jobs.html

Aerospace Engineering
asme.org/Jobs
aiaa.org/content.cfm?pageid=336 (for AIAA members only)

Agricultural Engineering
asabe.org/membership/career.html

Automotive Engineering
asme.org/Jobs
saecareercenter.org

Biomedical Engineering
http://careers.bmes.org/home/index.cfm?site_id=135
asme.org/Jobs
bmenet.org/BMEnet/db?action=list_by_keyword&keyword=job&
   ncolumns=1
aiha.org/EmploymentService/html/employmentservicehome.htm

Chemical Engineering
aiche.org/careerservices
acs.org/careers
vv-vv.com/awwa/U63848OR.cfm
jobtarget.com/home/index.cfm?site_id=128

Civil Engineering
http://careers.asce.org
adda.org/content/blogsection/9/46
jobtarget.com/home/index.cfm?site_id=128
vv-vv.com/awwa/U63848OR.cfm

Computer Engineering
aeanet.org/AboutAeA/EmpOpps.asp
acm.org/crc

Computer Science
aeanet.org/AboutAeA/EmpOpps.asphttp://asis.org
/careers.html
acm.org/crc

Electrical Engineering
http://ieee.org/web/careers/home/index.html
http://jobsconnection.sme.org/home/index.cfm?site_id=123
aeanet.org/AboutAeA/EmpOpps.asp
http://appanet.org/applications/classifieds/classifiedlist.cfm?sn.Item
Number=2049
acm.org/crc
energyvortex.com/careercenter
http://aesp.org/jobbankdisplaylistings.cfm
http://appanet.org/applications/classifieds/classifiedlist.cfm?sn.Item
Number=2049

Environmental Engineering
.aeesp.org
aiche.org/careerservices
http://careers.asce.org
wef.org/careeropps
aiha.org/EmploymentService/html/employmentservicehome
.htm
vv-vv.com/awwa/U63848OR.cfm
http://aesp.org/jobbankdisplaylistings.cfm
http://careers.aegweb.org

Facilities Engineering
jobtarget.com/home/index.cfm?site_id=128
appa.org/jobs/Arch/archindex.html

Industrial Engineering
iienet2.org/Landing.aspx?id=388
http://jobsconnection.sme.org/home/index.cfm?site_id=123
ashe.org
jobtarget.com/home/index.cfm?site_id=128

Manufacturing Engineering
http://jobsconnection.sme.org/home/index.cfm?site_id=123
jobtarget.com/home/index.cfm?site_id=128

Materials Science and Engineering
asnt.org/marketplace/helpwanted/helpwanted.htm
http://careercenter.asminternational.org/search.cfm
ceramics.org/membership/JobCenter/jobpostingsactivities.asp (members only)

Mechanical Engineering
http://jobsconnection.sme.org/home/index.cfm?site_id=123
asme.org/jobs
ans.org/career
asnt.org/marketplace/helpwanted/helpwanted.htm
jobtarget.com/home/index.cfm?site_id=128
aeevshow.com/classifieds
http://aesp.org/jobbankdisplaylistings.cfm

Mining Engineering
miningjobs.org
tms.org/Society/careers.html

Nuclear Engineering
ans.org/career
aeevshow.com/classifieds
http://aesp.org/jobbankdisplaylistings.cfm

Petroleum Engineering
http://careers.aegweb.org
spe.org/spe-app/spe/index.jsp

Structural Engineering
seaint.org/seaemp1.asp
http://careers.asce.org
jobtarget.com/home/index.cfm?site_id=128

General Engineering
http://jobsconnection.sme.org/home/index.cfm?site_id=123
aiha.org/EmploymentService/html/employmentservicehome.htm
jobtarget.com/home/index.cfm?site_id=128

aeevshow.com/classifieds
engcen.com/turbo/entry.htm

Engineering Co-op and Internships
tech-interns.com
ieeeusa.org/careers/student.menu.html
gomr.mms.gov/homepg/recruit/___Student_Programs/Engineering
  _Internships/engineering_internships.html
diversitycareers.com/articles/college/sumfall03/fot_coops.htm

General Career Information
http://library.dialog.com/bluesheets/html/bloC.html#CODIR
barrons.com
careerjournal.com
hoovers.com

Despite the ease of access to information on the Internet, it is worth repeating that the Internet should not be your only source of information. There is so much available in print as well. You owe it to yourself to become familiar with the important resources available in your university career center and the library. A short list follows:

General Reference Material
Dun & Bradstreet (dnb.com)
Standard and Poor's Register of Corporations, Directors and Executives
  (standardandpoors.com)
Directory of American Research and Technology
The Corporate Directory of U.S. Public Companies
Ward's Business Directory of Corporate Affiliations
Ward's Business Directory of U.S. Private and
  Public Companies

Area Trends in Employment
The People's Almanac's Book of Lists
Dictionary of Occupational Titles
Moody's Reference Manuals
Moody's Industrial Manual
Moody's International Manual
Business Phone Book USA: The National Directory of Addresses and
  Telephone Numbers
The Directory of Directories

The following is a list of reference materials that contain descriptions of companies you may want to use in your job search. Some of these references are material supply catalogs that have company listings within them (usually toward the back) that describe the products that the companies manufacture.

The Biotechnology Information Directory (cato.com/biotech)
ChemcyclopediaCorp Tech Directory of Technology Companies
Corp Tech Fast 5000 Company Locator
Directory of American Research and Technology
Job Choices in Science and Industry
Laser Focus World Buyer's Guide
Materials Engineering
Modern Plastics Encyclopedia
Nuclear News
Plastics Technology
Research and Development Directory

Specific Company Information

The websites of the specific companies that interest you are also a source of valuable information. However, you need to remember that this is only the information the employer wants you to have. To be well prepared, you also need to research more objective sources of information about the organization in which you are interested. Both the print and Internet sources previously mentioned can help you in this regard.

For publicly traded companies, the annual report is an extremely helpful piece of information and will usually be available online. And you do not have to be an M.B.A. to read it for your purposes!

Begin by reading the chief executive officer's letter to shareholders. It will address the challenges and the achievements of the company in the past year. It will also describe a plan of action for the future. The plan will indicate how employees will be impacted by the plan.

Next you should look at the gross sales and the expenditures. Are there any areas that appear to be larger than expected, or significantly higher than the previous year? This may be a good source of questions about what was going on within the company to require such costs.

Acquisitions and new product lines might also be identified in reading the annual report. It is a wealth of information and could help you in gaining an edge in the interview process.

More company information is available by accessing databases such as CAREER SEARCH, ABI/Inform, Compact Disclosure, and Newspaper Abstracts. Generally, these databases can be accessed online through your Internet server or through your college career services office and/or university library.

Identifying Job Openings for Engineers

Engineering majors tend to be well served by their campus career services offices. It is advisable to register with that office as soon as possible and use all of the resources that it makes available. The National Association of Colleges and Employers, the primary professional association for college and university career services directors and corporate recruiters, annually publishes a series entitled Job Choices, with a special volume for engineers. This is must reading for engineering students planning to enter the job market.

Specialized listings also are available through contacting the various engineering professional associations and societies. You will find contact information at the end of this chapter.

Possible Employers

There are numerous listings and rankings of companies. These companies provide excellent career opportunities for engineers. For example, the website manufacturing.net classifies various companies under specific industry titles as follows:

Aerospace and Defense
Boeing Corp.
Lockheed Martin Corp.
Northrop Grumman Corp.
Raytheon Co.
Rockwell International Corp.
Textron Inc.

Automotive
Barnes Group Inc.
Ford Motor Co.
General Motors Corp.

Goodyear Tire and Rubber Co.
Toyota
Honda
BMW

Communication and Utilities
AT&T Corp.
Baldor Electric Co.
Emerson Electric Co.
Koninklijke Philips Electronics
MCI

Metals and Chemicals
Dow Chemical Co.
Exxon Mobil Corp.
Minnesota Mining and Manufacturing Co. (3M)
PPG Industries
Sherwin-Williams Co.
United States Steel Corp.

Logistics and Supply Chain Management
Columbus McKinnon Corp.
Federal Express Corp.
WW Grainger Inc.
Hughes Supply Inc.
Parker Hannifin Corp.
Ryder Systems Inc.
UPS
Yellow Corp.

Technology
Apple Computer Inc.
Dell Inc.
Hewlett Packard Co.
Honeywell International Inc.
Intel Corp.
Microsoft Corp.
Motorola Inc.
National Instruments Corp.
National Semiconductor Corp.

Oracle Corporation
Sun Microsystems Inc.
Texas Instruments Inc.

Diversified Companies
Eaton Corp.
GE
Ingersoll Rand Co.

Opportunities in Small and Midsize Companies

There is a growing number of opportunities for new engineers in small and midsize companies. Those who have an entrepreneurial spirit and want to "see it all" will find exciting opportunities in this job sector. Often the remuneration is lower than in a big company, but the potential payoff can be extremely high when the company does well.

Many emerging companies are started by an individual or a group of individuals with special expertise that is needed in a specific industry or many industries. These companies enter into a contractual agreement with businesses and industries to supply the goods or services as an outside vendor. The relationship generally results in lower costs for the business or industry customer and increased profits for the small or midsize company. As the demand for these companies' products and services increases they will seek to add engineering staff to keep pace with their growing markets. When managed correctly, these companies can become the conglomerates of the future. However, it is still important to research them well because if they do not make it you could be out of a job faster, and with less security, than if you were with a large organization. Here are some suggestions:

• **Research the owner's background and reputation through local professional organizations, the local chamber of commerce, and the local newspaper.** It is easy to run a check of any articles that may have been written about this person. Who's Who publications also give a complete profile of distinguished and accomplished people in the profession and/or the locality.

• **Most schools or colleges of engineering have "industrial relations" programs.** Contact them to see if the company has participated in any of their programs. Try to use this source to learn as much as you can about the company's goals, challenges, and needs.

• **Research the technology and/or the process.** Does the company or owner(s) hold the patents for their technology? Are there any challenges to the patents? Is the technology in demand or is it being phased out? Is the technology needed by a broad spectrum of industries or does it fit a niche market? What are the projections for that market? Who is the competition and who are the customers?

• **Are there any financial records available for review?** Are contracts with customers multiyear or single year? What happens at the end of the contract?

It pays to be cautious, but the challenge and excitement of being part of a growing company is something that should be seriously considered. After you have conducted your in-depth research and concluded that this is an opportunity to grow with the company, give it your all. The rewards can be well worth it.

Possible Job Titles

The functional areas identified earlier can be used to categorize the myriad of job titles in the field of engineering. For example, a "reliability engineer" can hold a degree in almost any engineering discipline, but such an engineer is almost always found in the "production" or "operations" area of any industry. This means that whether the reliability engineer is employed in manufacturing, mining, or construction, he or she has responsibility for the methods, procedures, and quality control to successfully complete a project or put a product on the market. Reliability engineers maintain or improve the design of a product to ensure that it performs as intended.

Other engineering job titles include:

• **Process engineers.** Develop the series of actions (processes) to efficiently and economically make products such as computers; consumer products; candies, food, and drink; fuel; pharmaceuticals; medical devices; chemicals and plastics; and energy.

• **Process controls engineers.** Use statistics and engineering knowledge to manage and control the output from a production or manufacturing process.

• **Product/production engineers.** Apply engineering knowledge to the manufacturing process and to the methods of production. They plan and develop the tools, processes, machines, and equipment necessary to produce or manufacture products, as well as integrate facilities and systems to produce high-quality products safely and economically.

- **Operations engineers.** Concerned with the flow of materials and information. They use statistical models to describe behavior and evaluate effectiveness of manufacturing, supply chain, and service systems.
- **Logistics engineers.** Deal with purchasing, transporting, storing, distributing and warehousing raw materials, unfinished, "work-in-process," and finished goods and products.
- **Manufacturing engineers.** Control the overall manufacturing process, including the processes and methods of production. They develop the plan for manufacturing.
- **Systems engineers.** Consider business and technical needs with the goal of providing a quality solution that meets specified needs of all parties. They integrate engineering disciplines and specialties to design a holistic process that proceeds from concept to production to distribution and disposal.
- **Quality engineers.** Test and inspect procedures, using metrology, statistical methods, and cost concepts and techniques. They diagnose and correct improper quality-control practices with MIS systems and audits to detect deficiencies and make corrections.
- **Design engineers.** Can be from almost every engineering discipline. They develop product concept and specifications and direct the design effort. They use input from sources such as manufacturing, purchasing, tool making, and packaging engineering.
- **Consulting engineers.** Represent the customer's interests. Within industry, consulting engineers bring specialized knowledge to different business groups to help them address such issues as launching new products or solving problems that are impeding production. In the area of software engineering, consulting engineers ensure that the software under development meets the needs of the customer. There are also consulting engineers who represent client interests with architects, builders, and other suppliers engaged on a construction project.
- **Materials management engineers.** Assist organizations in managing inventory using strict controls and monitoring procedures from request to purchase to disposal. They also use forecasting and simulation models to solve inventory and control problems, as well as warehousing and transportation issues.
- **Applications engineers.** Engage in technical sales. They provide assurances to clients that the product will meet the client requirements. After the sale of the product, applications engineers assist in the integration of the product into the client's setting or help to solve a problem with the product.

- **Field engineers.** Interact with clients on a daily basis to provide engineering or project-management services. They can also be involved in the installation of equipment at client sites, similar to applications engineers.

Related Occupations

In addition to job titles directly related to engineering, engineers work in numerous areas. These areas benefit from the expertise and mind-set that engineers bring to the job. Some of these related areas include the following.

Marketing and Sales

Sales engineers or technical representatives sell complex products and services that require a technical background to understand the product and the customer needs. Applications engineers are the technical experts who support the product, make recommendations for further development and/or improvement of the product, or develop applications for the customer.

Production

Occupational specialties are named according to the technology with which they are most closely associated (e.g., chemical engineer, mining engineer, biomedical engineer). They may also be associated with the system or product that they engineer (e.g., control systems design engineer). Manufacturing engineers specify how the product will be produced. Production engineers design the production scheme. Reliability engineers work in both the product development and manufacturing stages to ensure that the product performs as it was intended. Field engineers are also involved in production activity when employed by consulting or technical services companies, such as contract construction firms. In these settings, field engineers may set up the plant or facility.

Technical Services

Process engineers are involved in maintaining, enhancing, and developing processes that support the overall engineering processes.

Research

Research engineers conduct basic, systematic investigations leading to new knowledge for a specific application. Development engineers, working with the research team, design, construct, and test prototypes and models. This can include setting up and operating pilot plants.

Information Systems Processing

Software applications engineers analyze, design, develop, and implement systems and networks central to the company or organization. Systems analysts examine the overall informational needs of the company or organization and design or recommend computer systems and networks that will address those needs.

Professional Associations

The following are specific professional associations for various industries that employ engineers:

American National Standards Institute (ANSI)
11 W. 42nd St., 13th Fl.
New York, NY 10036
ansi.org

Applied Research Laboratories
The University of Texas at Austin
P.O. Box 8029
Austin, TX 78713-8029
arlut.utexas.edu

Association for Facilities Engineers (AFE)
Formerly the American Institute of Plant
    Engineers (AIPE)
8180 Corporate Park Dr., Ste. 305
Cincinnati, OH 45242
jobtarget.com/home/index.cfm?site_id=128

Association of Home Appliance Manufacturers (AHAM)
20 N. Wacker Dr., Ste. 12311
Chicago, IL 60606
aham.org

Association of Industrial Manufacturers' Representatives (AIM/R)
222 Merchandise Mart, Ste. 1360
Chicago, IL 60654
aimr.net

Certified Ballast Manufacturers (CBM)
355 Lexington Ave., 17th Fl.
New York, NY 10017-6603
certbal.org

Electrical Manufacturing & Coil Winding Association, Inc. (EMCWA)
P.O. Box 278
Imperial Beach, CA 91933
emcwa.org

Gas Appliance Manufacturers Association (GAMA)
1901 N. Moore St., Ste. 1100
Arlington, VA 22209
gamanet.org

Industrial Distribution Association (IDA)
3 Corporate Square, Ste. 201
Atlanta, GA 30329
ida-assoc.org

Manufacturers' Agents National Association (MANA)
23016 Mill Creek Rd.
P.O. Box 3467
Laguna Hills, CA 92654-3467
manaonline.org

Motor and Equipment Manufacturers' Association
P.O. Box 13966
Research Triangle Park, NC 27709-3966
mema.org

National Electrical Manufacturers Association (NEMA)
1300 N. 17th St., Ste. 1847
Rosslyn, VA 22209
nema.org

National Electrical Manufacturers Representatives Association (NEMRA)
200 Business Park Dr., Ste. 301
Armonk, NY 10504
nemra.org

Society of Manufacturing Engineers (SME)
1 SME Dr.
P.O. Box 930
Dearborn, MI 48121-0930
sme.org

Society Plastics Industry, Inc. (SPI)
1801 K St., NW, Ste. 600K
Washington, DC 20006
socplas.org

Many professional associations serve the needs of every engineering discipline and functional area.

7

Path 2: Consulting

Contributions to this chapter were made by David Siegel, National Society of Professional Engineers.

According to *Webster's Dictionary*, a consultant is defined as "one who gives expert advice." Historically, engineers have been sought as consultants for projects ranging from the ancient pyramids in Egypt to the Panama Canal, from the space shuttle to everyday consumer products such as cell phones and laptop computers and software that runs major corporations. Today, business, industry, and government all seek engineering consultants to solve problems related to competitiveness, efficiency, environmental life cycles and high-rise construction. As in the past, the expertise of engineers is needed to address and solve today's human and technological challenges. Engineering consultants are often the most efficient and economical professionals to address myriad issues including the reclamation of the environment, the design or redesign of various products and processes, the restoration and improvement of transportation systems, and manufacturing competitiveness.

Consulting engineers work in a wide range of areas, and their success is usually very dependent on both the technical and the entrepreneurial skills of the individual engineer. In the past, many engineers did not consider a career in consulting until they had several years of experience in some relevant type of work. Today, however, consulting engineering companies are frequent recruiters in college career services offices. Because of the long hours and heavy travel demands, these organizations find that entry-level engineers can perform the basic support functions that senior consultants need in today's complex economy. Consulting offers the opportunity to work with highly intelligent colleagues and to experience a number of different challenges for a wide variety of clients.

Definition of the Career Path

It used to be that when people thought of consulting engineers, what often came to mind were consultants on construction projects such as highways, bridges, and high-rise and other complex buildings. However, today's manufacturers seek design consultants to develop new products or improve existing products; or they seek information technology consultants to implement new software applications to manage human resources, marketing, and/or accounting functions. Service and manufacturing businesses have begun seeking the technical expertise of engineers as they strive to become more efficient in their overall operations. Some of the issues for which business and industry seek engineering consultants include e-commerce and e-business solutions, cutting time to release new products, and reducing inventory. Consultants also assist in eliminating nonproductive elements of doing business, such as:

Time to complete work in process
Cycle times from conceptualization to market
Manufacturing delays due to downtime
Nonhazardous waste disposal
Inventory cost savings

While the responsibilities and challenges vary widely, there tend to be three types of consulting organizations for which engineers work.

1. **Consulting engineering firm.** These firms tend to employ specific types of engineers for specific purposes. A good example of this type of consulting firm would be MWH Engineering Company (mwhglobal.com), which works in the areas of energy, infrastructure, water, and wastewater.
2. **Design consulting firm.** These organizations are hired by major corporations to redesign existing products or design new concept products such as cell phones or roller blades. Companies such as IDEO (ideo.com) and Hertz LaZar Bell, Inc. (hlb.com) are examples of this type of consulting firm.
3. **Management consulting firm.** These firms are hired by corporations to perform tasks such as the design and implementation of information systems to manage such things as payroll, accounting, or supply chain. Increasingly, these firms are involved in developing e-commerce and e-business solutions.

Management consulting firms are as diverse as the engineering disciplines themselves. As a result, consulting careers offer an unlimited variety of opportunities for personal growth and development. Doing your research on the type of clients or engagements for which consulting firms hire entry-level engineers is very important. It is also important to learn the potential career development opportunities for entry-level engineers. It is also important to know what percentage of new hires, who remain with the firm, make that career progression that the company describes.

With the proliferation of international, national, regional, and local environmental regulations, environmental compliance has created many opportunities for consulting engineers. Environmental consulting firms provide services ranging from site assessment to design and construction for environmental compliance. There is strong demand for *environmental and chemical engineering consulting* services. At international environmental consulting firms such as Camp Dresser & McKee (cdm.com), engineers are involved in projects to help municipalities better use their water supply or restore and expand transportation sites. They can also be involved in the design of offshore landfill projects for domestic or foreign governments. As consultants, environmental engineers can become involved in diverse projects related to land reclamation, wastewater treatment, solid and hazardous waste disposal, storm water management, or noise abatement.

Computer science and computer engineering consultants provide an array of services to both corporate and government clients. This type of consulting engineer applies his or her knowledge to such projects as e-commerce, client-server development, database development, or computer networking design. Others may actually manage the technological assets of their clients. These consulting positions require continuing education as clients look for computer consultants with the most up-to-date knowledge of specific computer hardware, programming languages, and software applications.

Product design consultants are involved in the initial stages of product development. They design and prototype and usually assess the manufacturability of a new product. Some consultants ultimately manage large-scale projects, including product and plant start-ups. In addition, consultants in this area solve material-processing problems; provide an interface with the market in which the product will be sold, including attracting new clients to the company; and conduct reliability, safety, and compliance testing under contract to a specific client or a group of clients.

Working Conditions

The consulting engineering career path requires a high degree of personal initiative and professional effort. Long hours and constant travel are hallmarks of this career path. However, this path offers unlimited opportunities for engineers to deal with different problems, organizational types, and personnel.

The challenge of interacting with different people in different environments is probably one of the most significant features of the engineering career path in the field of consulting. It distinguishes it from the engineering career path in industry, government, or academia. This does not mean that variety does not exist in the other engineering career paths. It simply means that consulting engineers must always expect change and diversity to be a regular part of their career. Consulting also provides an excellent exposure to a wide variety of businesses and industries. In addition, there are many people to learn from and many people to get to know.

Consulting engineers often deal with personnel who represent different levels of authority and competency within their own organization, as well as within the client's organization. Consulting engineers must have the ability to interact with all levels of authority and competence in order to bring each project to a successful conclusion.

Another phenomenal resource that engineers in the consulting industry have is their own colleagues. Consulting engineers on the whole have a relatively high degree of education. In addition, they are all proficient in at least one major area of the business activity. This exposure to a very diverse set of competent individuals is a tremendous asset to the professional development of consulting engineers. It provides a background that the consultant can utilize to analyze future problems.

The Relationship with Clients

It is important to remember that the role of a consulting engineer is one of service. It is not enough for an engineer in this area to keep up with the latest techniques in his or her discipline. Consulting engineers must also possess the ability to apply objectivity, experience, understanding, and time to the solution of each client's problems. Above all, the recommended solution must fit the client's own environment. This is often the most difficult challenge that engineering consultants face.

Consultants not only have to recommend the correct solution but also one that the client can implement. Making a recommendation that cannot be implemented by the client can quickly lead to client dissatisfaction. In fact, doing so can be very similar to making an inaccurate recommendation.

This aspect of consulting is often a challenge and an education for the new consulting engineer. The new engineer has been trained in the latest techniques and educated in the appropriate engineering theory. He or she knows that the recommendations are theoretically or technically correct. However, if they do not meet the expectations or needs of the client, those recommendations may be totally useless.

In the end, a correct solution but a dissatisfied client is lost business to the consulting firm and a setback in the career of a consulting engineer. It is important to remember that in consulting only two things matter: the quality of one's work and the satisfaction of one's clients!

Schedule and Travel Demands

All consultants work at the discretion of their clients. Therefore they must work at peak performance at all times. This is particularly true for consulting engineers. The nature of their work often requires unpredictable and unlimited time commitments. Consultants are often brought in during crisis situations. They are expected to do whatever it takes to solve the problem. In other words, one cannot rest until a solution is found.

It is such situations that can lead consulting engineers to feel that their time may not be their own. The pressure of deadlines and the extensive amount of travel required are factors that govern the professional lives of consulting engineers.

Certainly the traveling aspect of consulting can be viewed as a disadvantage. It can also be viewed as a broadening feature. Travel provides exposure to a wide range of cultures and lifestyles and can be a real advantage for the engineer in consulting. Nonetheless, there is a negative side to considerable travel. One has to be able to adjust to it, particularly in one's personal life.

Consulting engineers typically work long hours, and the time spent away from home can be significant. The inability to adjust to these realities can create unsatisfactory personal situations and adversely affect the consultant's work. Therefore, it is not surprising that travel and the demands that it makes on one's personal life are the major reasons why individuals leave the consulting profession. That is why more and more consulting firms are making significant strides in addressing "quality of work life" issues.

Education and Qualifications

A strong engineering background at the bachelor's level provides a fundamental basis for entering the consulting profession. It is difficult to advance in some areas without an M.B.A. from one of the top schools.

In the last three to five years there has been an increase in the number of consulting firms seeking to hire individuals with Ph.D.s or master's degrees in engineering. Some of the world's largest management consulting firms have recently begun to recruit and hire engineering Ph.D.s in the same manner as they recruit and hire M.B.A. graduates. These firms have found that Ph.D.s have been trained to identify problems, devise ways to solve them, and incorporate new information while thinking on their feet. These are exactly the characteristics that make Ph.D. hires a good match for the client needs of major management consulting firms. As a result, there are Ph.D. engineers who become strong and effective management consultants. Today, their starting salaries equal or exceed those of M.B.A.s. In fact, their salaries are usually in the six figures, particularly for those who are fluent in foreign languages. There is also a new demand for the graduates of combined graduate programs of engineering and business administration, such as the programs at Northwestern University, MIT, Stanford, Michigan, and Carnegie Mellon.

There are many different areas of activity in consulting, and all of these areas require an understanding of both technical and operational problems. While a degree in engineering is a particularly useful background, experience in industry is extremely helpful, particularly experience in the manufacturing sector. Manufacturing industries represent a significant portion of consulting clients. Consulting firms of all types look for entry-level engineers who have gained insight into the functions, needs, and challenges that face manufacturers. This type of experience is typically gained through undergraduate programs such as co-op, multi-summer internships, or full- or part-time work experience during college.

Industry experience helps entry-level engineers contribute to the formulation of more realistic recommendations that can be implemented by the client. In addition, the experience helps a consulting engineer to be sensitive to the problems associated with the operation of a profitable business. After all, the primary responsibilities of a consultant are problem solving and making recommendations. However, it's important to remember that once the job ends and the recommendations are made, execution of the recommendations rests with the client.

Professional Licensing of Consulting Engineers

Most consulting engineers need to become a registered or licensed engineer in the state where they work. Once licensed, these engineers are known as "professional engineers" and are permitted to put the designation "PE" after their names. Professional licensure means that the engineer has completed a certain level and type of engineering education and has demonstrated through both professional experience and examination a specific level of competency in a field of engineering. There are four steps to becoming a PE:

1. Graduate from an accredited engineering curriculum. (Engineering curricula are accredited by the Accreditation Board of Engineering and Technology [ABET]).
2. Pass the Fundamentals of Engineering exam (FE).
3. Obtain four years of engineering experience, although this can vary by state.
4. Pass the Principles and Practice of Engineering exam (PPE), once the minimum years of engineering experience have been obtained.

Why would an engineer go through such a rigorous process? It is widely held that the PE license increases opportunities for hiring, promotion, and professional development. This is particularly true in an increasingly global economy. In addition, there are some positions that can only be held by PEs.

- Only a PE can prepare, sign and seal, and submit engineering plans and drawings to a public authority for approval, or seal engineering work for public and private clients.
- Some states require that individuals teaching engineering or engineering design courses be licensed.
- Consulting engineers or private practitioners find the PE designation to be invaluable in bidding on and securing contracts.
- Some government agencies require that certain higher-level engineers be licensed.

Regardless of whether or not the PE license is a requirement in a specific engineering career path, it is important to keep in mind that if you are among a group of candidates for an open position and each of you is considered to be equally qualified, the one who has a PE license is most likely to be deemed the best choice for the position. That individual has met a standard of excellence that is documented for the employer.

Some engineers think that licensure is not necessary for those involved with industry. However, according to the website Manufacturing.Net, PEs working as plant engineers command higher salaries than their counterparts without licensure.

It is possible in today's economy that it will become necessary to be licensed in more than one state. Despite some variation, due to local laws and regulations, most states have the same general requirements for licensure. This allows for a process called reciprocity, which means that an engineer can be licensed in more than one state without further examination.

To hold multistate licensure, the standards of each state must equal a minimum standard. It is important to consult the state licensing board in each state in which licensure will be sought, to make sure that all requirements are met. Remember that licensure laws are exclusively under the control of individual state legislatures.

To maintain one's PE license, continuing education may be required. At this writing, fifteen states require PEs to complete additional education for relicensure. These are called Continuing Professional Competency (CPC) rules. The rules vary from state to state, but, in general, PEs are required to complete fifteen professional development hours (PDHs) per year. These hours can be acquired through different types of activities, including course work, as stipulated by the state. See the Appendix for a list of state examining boards.

Additional information about professional licensure can be obtained from:

The National Council of Examiners for Engineering and Surveying (NCEES), ncees.org
NCEES list of state licensure boards, ncees.org/licensure/licensing_boards
Professional Publications online resources, ppi2pass.com
American Council of Engineering Companies, acec.org

Combined Programs of Study

In addition to the PE license, experienced consulting engineers often return to school for either a master's in business administration or in engineering. Unique graduate programs are offered, such as the Project Management master's degree at Northwestern University, and combined programs of business and engineering at the graduate level can also be found at MIT, Stanford, Michigan, Northwestern, and Carnegie Mellon. Graduates of these programs join large corporations and management consulting firms.

Today it is becoming increasingly necessary for engineers in the consulting industry to couple their technical background with graduate education in business. In fact, after three to five years in the industry, a master's degree in business (M.B.A.) is almost a necessity. Anyone who desires to enter the consulting profession would certainly need to prepare to pursue post-graduate work in business administration or an associated field of study on a part-time or full-time basis at some point during his or her career.

Of course, this type of formal educational background does not automatically qualify one for entry into or promotion within the consulting industry. It is, however, a very definite advantage. In addition, continuing professional development courses, whether offered in-house or on university campuses, are necessities for consulting engineers to stay current in their fields.

Earnings

Consulting engineering has had a reputation for being a highly selective field that offers high levels of compensation to entry-level engineers. While industry salaries have tended to catch up to consulting salaries, it is important to know that starting salaries in consulting firms vary widely depending on the skills and knowledge you bring. In addition, consulting engineering firms usually provide excellent training and educational benefits to ensure that their consultants are knowledgeable and competent in the latest theory and techniques.

According to *Careers in Consulting* (careers-in-business.com/consulting/mcsal.htm), bachelor's-level consultants can receive starting salaries ranging from $40,000 to $80,000, with engineers being toward the upper end, if they have industry experience. Some bachelor-level hires also receive bonuses of $5,000 to $10,000. Graduates of combined engineering and management programs can typically command six figures and may be offered signing bonuses and other enticements to join major consulting firms. Increasingly, Ph.D. candidates in engineering are being recruited by consulting firms, and their starting salaries are typically as high as the graduate salary mentioned above.

There is ample opportunity for economic growth in the consulting field, as evidenced by the more successful consultants in the industry today. The consultant's compensation is equivalent to and sometimes surpasses the economic reward of an engineer in industry. However, the rate of salary increases, once employed, will depend on the individual's ability to contribute to projects.

While the selectivity and the high compensation are attractive features of the engineering consulting career path, the long hours and intensive pressure to meet deadlines are sometimes seen as the disadvantages of this career path. Often, the consulting engineer must work in a manner—and on a schedule—that is prescribed by the client. This may mean that the engineer's time is not his or her own and, unfortunately, compensation alone is the "just reward."

Career Outlook

Many consulting opportunities exist for engineers, and more are expected to emerge as industry "outsources" more and more engineering functions. Carol Kleinman, the syndicated columnist and author of numerous books on the job market, reports that "engineers will be in so much demand that private engineering consulting firms will boom." Likewise, *The American Almanac of Jobs and Salaries* reports that "a major source of engineering jobs exists in consulting firms." It appears that the outlook is bright for this career path in terms of future growth and expansion.

After several years with a large or midsize consulting company, some engineers may leave to start their own consulting firms. In recent years a number of engineers who have been in industry have left to form consulting firms and now sell their services back to their former employers.

Strategy for Finding the Jobs

Employers of consulting engineers look for candidates who demonstrate the following characteristics:

- Experience related to the needs of their major clients
- Knowledge of the basic technical and software tools of the industry
- Exceptional analytical abilities
- A willingness to work in a competitive environment
- High levels of personal motivation
- The ability to work independently, as well as part of a team
- Strong interpersonal skills

If you are trying to determine if you are a strong candidate for a consulting firm, it is advisable to assess whether or not you:

- Have solid technical knowledge needed by the organization(s) to which you are applying
- Have strong quantitative abilities
- Have outstanding social skills and leadership abilities

- Are comfortable with ambiguity
- Are able to reach conclusions that faculty and/or supervisors consider to be accurate, even when you do not have enough time or information
- Are flexible
- Are able and willing to travel
- Are able and willing to work eighty-plus hours a week

Your Consulting Résumé

If you feel you are a strong candidate for a consulting firm, it will be important to restructure your engineering résumé when presenting yourself to consulting firms. First, you will want to significantly condense your background and stress the skills that are important to the type of consulting firm to which you are applying. For example, instead of describing the technical aspect of a project that you undertook as part of one of your co-op assignments, reword the description to show that you "managed a subset of tasks necessary to reduce the cost of manufacturing" or "participated on a team to increase productivity of an offshore facility" or "led a group of warehouse workers to analyze inventory problems and propose solutions to upper management."

To make sure that your descriptions are well targeted for the company to which you will be applying, visit the company's website in order to learn what skills they seek for entry-level positions held by engineers.

The only exception to this advice is when your résumé is being sent to a consulting firm that is involved in specific technical work such as biomedical engineering, environmental engineering, or civil engineering. In these cases, the company will want to know the specific technical knowledge that you can bring to the organization immediately. For example, if you are a biomedical engineer and you have worked for a small medical device developer, you will want to show, for example, that you have conducted quality assurance testing, or computerized design specifications for device parts, or prepared FDA reports. In these cases, it will be important to not only emphasize your technical skills but also your technical work experience. Reading the firm's online job descriptions will help you know what to emphasize on your résumé.

If you are applying to management consulting firms, you will also need to know how to participate in a very special type of job interview called a "case interview." In a case interview, one or more members of the consulting firm describes a business problem to you and asks for your solution. The purpose of this type of interview is to demonstrate how you structure your thinking to approach such a problem. There are expected approaches (not answers) to this type of interview, and you will need to be well prepared and trained in how to handle case interviews if you want to successfully compete for consulting positions. There are numerous resources available to you for learning this process. You should begin in your career services office and also use the resources provided in this chapter.

There are many online resources for learning about careers in consulting such as:

careers-in-business.com
career.cornell.edu/students/explore/careerbriefs/mgmtconsult
.html
alsa.asn.au/careers/directry/alt/2001/manage.htm
wetfeet.com/research/industries/consulting/home.asp
stern.nyu.edu/consulting/Careers/Career_Choices.html
Chamber of Commerce directories (these can be located online)

The websites of major consulting firms can also be very helpful in learning not only about the firm but also about consulting careers in general. There are numerous other resources for preparing for the consulting career path.

Dun and Bradstreet's *Million Dollar Directory*
The Business of Consulting: The Basics and Beyond, Elaine Biech
Management Consulting: A Complete Guide to the Industry, Sugata Biswas
    and Daryl Twitchell
"So You Want To Be a Consultant: Some Tips on How To Prepare,"
    Andrew Fusscas (an article from *Review of Business*)
Killer Consulting Résumés: The WetFeet.com Insider Guide, WetFeet.com,
    Wet Feet Press
Ace Your Case! Consulting Interviews: The WetFeet.com Insider Guide, Wet
    Feet Press, Gary Alpert, Steve Pollock, WetFeet.com
The Wharton MBA Case Interview Study Guide, Volumes I and II,
    Wharton MBA Students, Wharton MBA Consulting Club
*Management Consulting: Exploring the Field, Finding the Right Job and
    Landing It!*, Convergence Multimedia and Harvard Business School
    Publishing
Consultants and Consulting Organizations Directory, Gale Research
Consultants News, Kennedy Publications
Directory of Management Consultants, Kennedy Publications

Harvard Business School Career Guide: Management Consulting, Harvard
   Business School Publishing
*The World's Newest Profession: Management Consulting in the Twentieth
   Century*, Christopher D. McKenna

Reference Materials

Researching the companies that offer opportunities related to your area(s) of
interest is the next step. There are additional resources that can assist you.

National Directory of Addresses and Telephone Numbers
The Directory of Directories
Dun's Directory of Consulting Firms
Directory of Professional Engineers in Private Practice

Technical journals and magazines associated with each engineering discipline are excellent resources for identifying consulting engineering opportunities. Some of these publications include:

Aviation Weekly and AviationWeek.com
Chemical Engineering News
Chemical & Engineering News
EDN Career News, for the electronics industry
Electrical World magazine
Genetic Engineering News
Graduating Engineer magazine
Graduating Engineer & Computer Careers magazine
Machine Design magazine
Mechanical Engineering magazine and *Mechanical Engineering* magazine
   Online memagazine.org
*Medical Plastics and Biomaterials: Materials Technology for Medical
   Products*
ENR magazine, published by McGraw-Hill Construction
Nuclear News magazine

Possible Employers

A wide variety of consulting firms, including large, midsize, and small companies, constitute a major source of engineering jobs. Some of the categories
into which these firms can be divided include:

- Construction firms
- Construction management firms
- Consulting firms—business services
- Consulting firms—technical services

According to T. K. Spring, the small to midsize firms, those with less than two hundred to three hundred employees, tend to be more stable than larger consulting firms, which are known for having "peaks and valleys" of contracts that cause swings in the number of layoffs of consulting staff.

Civil and Environmental Engineering Consulting Firms
Bechtel (bechtel.com)
Black & Veatch (bv.com)
Camp Dresser & McKee (cdm.com)
CH2M Hill (ch2m.com/corporate)
Environ Corporation (environcorp.com)
Fluor Corporation (fluor.com)
Foth & Van Dyke and Associates, Inc. (foth.com)
Graef, Anhalt, Schloemer & Associates, Inc. (gasai.com)
Halliburton (halliburton.com/kbr/kbr.asp)
MWH (Montgomery Watson Harza) (mwhglobal.com)
Parsons Brinckerhoff Quade & Douglas, Inc. (pbworld.com)
HDR, Inc. (hdrinc.com)
O'Brien & Gere Engineers, Inc. (obg.com)
Parsons Inc. (parsons.com)
Sargent & Lundy (sargentlundy.com)
The Shaw Group, Inc. (shawgrp.com)
Jacobs Technology, Inc. (jacobstechnology.com)
URS Corporation (urscorp.com/main.htm)

Biomedical Engineering Consulting Firms
ARTECH Testing (artechlab.com)
Computer Aided Engineering Associates, Inc.
    (caeai.com/index.html)
Packer Engineering Inc. (packereng.com)

Computer Science and Engineering Consulting Firms
COMDISCO (comdisco.com)
Computer Associates, Inc. (cai.com)
IBM (ibm.com/us)

Microsoft Consulting Services (microsoft.com/services/microsoftservices /default.mspx)

Morgan Stanley Information Technology (morganstanley.com)

Management Consulting Firms

Accenture (accenture.com)

A.T. Kearney (atkearney.com)

The Boston Consulting Group (bcg.com)

Deloitte Consulting LLP (deloitte.com/dtt/section_node/0,1042,sid %253D26551,00.html)

Ernst & Young (ey.com)

Hewitt Associates (hewitt.com)

Kurt Salmon Associates (kurtsalmon.com)

McKinsey & Company (mckinsey.com)

Mercer Consulting (mercer.com)

PricewaterhouseCoopers (pwcglobal.com)

ZS Associates (zsassociates.com)

Product and Industrial Design Consulting Firms

Dynamic Group Circuit Design, Inc. (dgcdinc.com)

Daedalus Excel (daed.com)

Herbst LaZar Bell (hlb.com)

IDEO (ideo.com)

KJM Design (kjm-designs.com)

Realized Technologies Inc. (realized.com)

Possible Job Titles

Some of the job titles that are common in the consulting industry are:

Structural engineering consultant

Construction engineering consultant

Manufacturing engineering consultant

Systems analyst

Network consultant

Industrial engineering consultant

Business analyst

Project manager

Construction manager

Related Occupations

In addition to working for consulting firms, engineers can also be employed by industry in a consulting capacity. Some companies have internal consulting divisions. The job titles most often associated with this type of employment are technical services engineer or applications engineer.

Corporations employ technical services or applications engineers to support their customer base. The primary responsibility of this group of engineers is to serve as a technical consultant to the company's customers. These engineers train clients to use products and/or technology and solve any problems that might occur in the use of the company's products. They also communicate customer concerns to design and production engineers within their own company so that the product can be modified or improved to meet the needs of the client. In some instances, new product ideas are also brought to the attention of the company in order to open new markets.

Professional Associations

Association of Consulting Engineers Council
1015 15th St. NW, Ste. 802
Washington, DC 20005
acec.org

Association for Consultancy and Engineering (ACE)
Alliance House
12 Caxton St.
London
SW1H 0QL
acenet.co.uk

Association of Management Consulting Firms
521 Fifth Ave.
New York, NY 10175-3598
amcf.org/index.asp

Institute of Management Consultants U.S. (IMC US)
2025 M St. NW, Suite 800
Washington, DC 20036-3309
imcusa.org

Management Consultancies Association (MCA)
60 Trafalgar Square
London
WC2N 5DS
mca.org.uk/mca

See the *Encyclopedia of Associations* for an extensive listing of international consulting engineering associations.

8

Path 3: Government

While the government sector has always been an excellent employer of engineers, the image of government employment has suffered significantly and as a result, many talented engineers have chosen the private sector over government service. Now there is a serious shortage of well-prepared, motivated engineers in government service and steps are being taken to attract and recruit the best and the brightest to engineering careers in government. As always, government careers offer excellent benefits and career opportunities that provide challenge and fulfillment.

In some instances, a government career is one of the best career paths for specific engineering disciplines. For example, the U.S. Department of Homeland Security (dhs.gov/xabout/careers) hires engineers to prevent terrorist attacks and minimize the impact of such attacks and natural disasters. Engineers in Homeland Security can also conduct terrorism-related research and development.

At the state level, departments of transportation throughout the country, in combination with the U.S. Army Corps of Engineers (usace.army.mil/ howdoi/employment.htm), have been the principal employers of civil engineers. Similarly, the Food and Drug Administration (fda.gov/jobs/engineer .htm) is an employer of engineers, as is the U.S. Department of Defense (defenselink.mil/other_info/careers.html). The Defense Department continues to employ the largest number of engineers in both civilian and enlisted positions for its agencies and installations throughout the world. And these are only a few of the hundreds of federal government agencies hiring engineers and computer scientists.

According to the U.S. Office of Personnel Management (OPM) (opm .gov), the federal government alone hires between two hundred thousand and three hundred thousand people annually. Of those hired, more than half are engineers. Engineers employed by the federal government work in areas from homeland security to aerospace technology to environmental protection. Their careers can involve interaction with private sector companies, colleges and universities, and foreign governments. There is not one typical path that engineers follow within the government system. Instead, there are many varied and exciting opportunities to work on the cutting edge of technology.

Individuals interested in working for a government agency are always advised to start their job search early and make sure they present themselves in a competitive manner. Most government agencies require job applicants to apply online. Personal résumés can be provided as well but they cannot be substituted for the online application process. It is important to become familiar with these forms and the best techniques for completing them. This book will address this important topic later in this chapter.

Definition of the Career Path

A wide variety of opportunities exist for engineers in the public sector. There are engineering positions in the legislative branch of government, such as the U.S. Office of Technology Assessment (gpo.gov/careers/index.html), which keeps Congress informed about technological advances and the U.S. Government Accountability Office (formerly known as the U.S. General Accounting Office), which studies how tax dollars are spent by the government and advises Congress and people in the executive branch of government about how to make government more effective and responsive (gao.gov/jobopp.htm).

However as mentioned previously, the majority of engineering positions are in the executive branch of government, which includes the Department of Defense, Department of Homeland Security, NASA, the U.S. Army Corps of Engineers, Department of Energy, Department of Transportation, and others. This division of opportunity also holds true at the state and municipal levels.

Careers in Federal Government

In general, the U.S. Department of Labor's levels of engineering are established by monitoring engineering employment in the private sector. This allows the federal government to define its engineering career paths to be consistent with business and industry. See Chapter 6 for a description of the five levels of engineering careers.

While the government offers a good career path within most agencies, it is nevertheless important to note that experience within the government, particularly in areas of aerospace technology (as in the Department of Defense or NASA) and government regulations (as in the Environmental Protection Agency, the Nuclear Regulatory Commission, and the Food and Drug Administration) can be excellent springboards for careers in the industry sector. Corporations that conduct extensive business with the government or must meet government regulations to bring their products to market, place a high value on experience, even co-op experience with those agencies, because the engineer's knowledge of the inner workings of the agency can be vital to the company's bottom line.

Careers at the State and Local Level

According to the U.S. Census Bureau, more than thirteen million people are employed in state government. There are also many opportunities at the county and city level. Competition might not be as rigorous for some of these positions as similar positions at the federal level. In addition, the career progression for engineers might also not be as uniform as it is on the federal level. This phenomenon is primarily due to regional and local differences. It is therefore important to educate yourself about the engineering career paths in the locality in which you are interested.

There are two resources that can help you determine the career path of engineers at the state and local level.

1. *State Administrative Officials Classified by Function*, from Council of State Governments: Organized by state and updated biennially, this publication provides the names and addresses of officials in each type of state administrative department.
2. *Municipal Year Book*, from International City Management Association: This publication lists the addresses of city and county administrative offices and departments and is updated annually.

In addition, the State and Local Government Internet Directory (state localgov.net/index.cfm) provides access to thousands of state, city, and county government agency websites. Other online sites for these types of jobs include:

govjobscentral.net
afciviliancareers.com/careers.asp

military.com/engineering (for veterans)
federaljobsearch.com (includes some state government jobs)
http://50statejobs.com/cities.html
govtjobs.com (includes city, county, and state jobs)

Working Conditions

As stated earlier, government careers can be very satisfying. While compensation may not always equal that found in the private sector, the fringe benefits associated with government employment are generally very good. In addition, the engineering work can often be on the "cutting edge." At the federal level, this is particularly true. Consider the opportunities in aerospace, intelligence, and defense agencies.

It is inaccurate to assume that government positions always have less pressure than positions in consulting firms or private industry. While the working conditions might seem different, you should be careful about stereotyping government employment in this manner. Many of these positions have just as much pressure, if not more, than positions in the private sector! For example, there are life-and-death issues facing engineers in a NASA control room at the time of a space shuttle liftoff or landing. This is generally not the case in many corporate work settings. Likewise, the engineers at the Federal Aviation Administration make daily airline commuter travel routine and safe through the accuracy and preciseness of their work. Therefore, before jumping to erroneous conclusions about work with the government, do your homework! You could be passing up an exciting and rewarding career path based on erroneous stereotypes.

Earnings

Both federal and state governments have established pay systems for their employees. In the federal government, the largest pay system is called the "General Schedule" (GS). Under this system, engineering and computer-related positions have special pay rates.

The federal government hires engineers on a special rating scale. It is known as the "Special Salary Rate Table: 0414" and can be found on the Web at (apps.opm.gov/ssr/tables/index.cfm?action=pickDate&SrTable_nr =0414). Salary levels are set for each GS grade level annually, so it's important to check the table to see what the current rate of pay is for each level.

If you are seeking an engineering position in the Federal government, you will qualify for either the GS-5 or GS-7 pay grade level at graduation. If you have been an undergraduate engineering co-op student and/or have an undergraduate grade point average (GPA) of 3.0 or higher, on a 4.0 scale, or are a member of an academic honor society, you might qualify for the GS-7 grade level based on "Superior Academic Achievement." If you have a master's degree, you might be eligible for the GS-9 grade level, and, if you have a doctoral degree, you might qualify for the GS-11 level.

While annual pay rates can be lower than those in industry, government agencies at both the state and federal level usually provide excellent benefits packages including life insurance, retirement plans, a variety of health insurance options, and paid leave. In addition, there have been instances where some federal agencies offered "signing bonuses," in addition to the annual salary, to uniquely qualified engineers. In one case, the "signing bonus" was $9,900 per year for three years. If you are in the position to consider such an offer, it is advisable to read the contract thoroughly to make sure that you understand and are comfortable with all of the conditions under which the bonus will be paid or stopped.

Federal leave policy currently provides generous personal (vacation) and sick leave per year. In addition, there is paid leave for ten national holidays. A good Web source for understanding the federal leave policy is opm.gov/oca/leave.

Career Outlook

The government sector is always looking for good engineers from almost every engineering discipline. Even when government hiring declines, engineers, computer scientists, and other technically educated professionals continue to find opportunities at all levels of government.

The Office of Management and Budget has predicted that the demand for engineers will increase significantly by the year 2010. While most engineering jobs are in the executive branch of the federal government (e.g., Department of Defense, Department of Energy, Department of Transportation), there will also be opportunities in the legislative and judicial branches of government owing to the increased use of information technology and other technical advances.

In the legislative branch, engineers can look to agencies such as the General Accounting Office, General Services Administration, and the Office of Technology Assessment for new opportunities. Likewise, the outlook is also improving at the state and local level as Congress has shifted responsibility for major government services out of Washington, D.C., and back to the states. State employment offices will have up-to-date information on the job outlook in your specific area of interest.

Strategy for Finding the Jobs

In recent years, the government has invested heavily in online advising and recruiting mechanisms to help you in your job search. The federal government's official jobs site is USAJobs (usajobs.gov). However, every federal agency has its own job site link on its home page. There are two ways to apply for engineering positions in the federal government. When you know the agency for which you want to work, go to that website and use the "Jobs" or "Careers" link and follow these steps to apply:

1. Search the current vacancies.
2. Once you have found a vacancy you want to apply for, click the "apply to this vacancy button."
3. Complete the online registration form by selecting the "new user" button and providing your personal and work history information, including your résumé. Answer vacancy-specific questions, which have been developed to determine your basic eligibility and the group of candidates who will be referred to the manager for consideration.
4. Submit appropriate paper documentation requested on the vacancy announcement. Instructions on how to submit documentation are provided in the vacancy announcement.
5. When you have finished answering the vacancy-specific questions, select the "Finish" button and wait for the transmittal confirmation screen.

When you want to see all possible engineering positions with the federal government, go directly to the USAJobs website (usajobs.gov). Any agency's announcement will link you back to the agency in order to apply online.

According to the USAJobs website, "paper applications are generally not accepted for vacancy announcements; however, exceptions can be made in extreme hardship cases. Applicants requesting an exception must contact the Human Resources Specialist listed in the vacancy announcement prior to the closing date." There are more helpful tips on how to use the USAJobs site more effectively at http://help.usajobs.opm.gov/jobseeker/jobsearch/#key word.

Creating and Attaching a Federal Résumé

When an open position in the federal government requires a résumé in addition to the online application, you will need to have one ready to attach. Therefore, preparing a federal government résumé is one of the first steps in seeking a government position.

Although similar in nature to a résumé used to apply for a job in the private sector, federal government résumés **must include** certain specific data that is not always required for other types of jobs. To receive proper consideration, please make sure your résumé includes all of the following information:

- Full name
- Mailing address
- E-mail address
- Campus and home telephone numbers as well as day/evening numbers and cell phone numbers (always include area codes)
- Education: Include the following information: high school (school name, city, state, date of diploma or GED), college/university (school name, city, state, major field of study, type of degree [B.S., M.S., M.Eng., Ph.D., etc.] and year received, total academic credits earned [indicate whether semester or quarter hours])
- Work experience: Include details on all paid and unpaid work experiences that are relevant to the job for which you are applying. List your most recent jobs first. For each job include: job title (and grade level, if it was a federal job), duties and accomplishments, employer's name and address, supervisor's name and telephone number, starting and ending dates (month and year), hours worked per week, salary
- Other qualifications: Include things such as job-related training courses, job-related skills (e.g., CAD, AutoMod, etc.), computer software/hardware skills, foreign language proficiency, job-related honors, awards, special accomplishments, publications, memberships in professional or honor societies, leadership activities, and performance awards

Before you submit your federal government résumé, make sure you have followed these dos and don'ts.

Do

- Develop your résumé using a word processing program such as Microsoft Word or WordPerfect.
- Make sure your résumé is easy to read and understand.
- Include all appropriate dates and make sure that they are in sequence.
- Address relevant experiences that coincide with the vacancy questions.
- Copy and paste your résumé into the online job application system that you are using. If you need to edit your résumé, make the edits in Microsoft Word or WordPerfect, and then reinsert your résumé into the online system.
- Use the résumé "check length" tool to avoid error messages. Some sites limit the number of characters, words, or pages that can be submitted. Be sure to follow the specific directions for the positions for which you are applying.

Don't

- Try to type, edit, or print your résumé on or from the online job application sites. First, make changes to your document in your word processing software (MSWord or WordPerfect) before reinserting the résumé online.
- Use large margins. Please keep white space to a minimum.
- Use fancy fonts, bold text, unusual formats, or graphics.

If a federal government résumé is required, it must be entered online by the specified closing date (deadline). The online system will automatically attach your résumé to your application.

Resources for Finding a Government Job

Recruiting information on obtaining an engineering position with the federal government is available from the Office of Personnel Management through the Internet site usajobs.opm.gov. In addition, books such as Lily Whiteman's *Get Hired! How to Land the Ideal Federal Job and Negotiate a Top Salary* and *Ten Steps to a Federal Job: Navigating the Federal Job System, Writing Federal Résumés, KSAs and Cover Letters with a Mission* by Kathryn K. Troutman and Laura Sachs are excellent resources.

The website Careers in Government (careersingovernment.com) is the oldest and largest site for finding jobs in government, education, and other public sector agencies. It is a clearinghouse of information and resources, as well as a listing of job openings in the public sector and abroad.

Federal Times Online is an independent weekly online newsletter that includes a career website (federaltimes.com/index.php?C=career_informa tion). It lists federal jobs not only in Washington, D.C., but also nationwide and overseas.

Pse-net.com is a comprehensive site of government jobs posted by the Public Service Employee Network. It is not only a guide to government and public service jobs but it also provides career information, civil service test resources, certification resources, and links to other career websites for federal, international, state, and local positions, as well as government jobs by job function.

Federal Jobs. Pse-net.com provides links to federal government jobs at all major government agencies. In addition, it provides links to Canadian and international government jobs.

Pse-net.com also provides information on civil service test guides, tips for completing the government's job application form, and links to other websites and databases such as:

- Federal government pay schedules at opm.gov/oca/payrates/index.htm
- FedWorld, a website of the U.S. Department of Commerce that provides a link to search for federal government jobs (www.ntis.gov/jobs/jobsearch.aspx)
- HRS Federal Job Search (hrsjobs.com), which charges a monthly fee to conduct federal job searches by occupation, pay, and location
- Military Career Guide Online (militarycareers.com), which provides details on enlisted and officer occupations in the armed services

Other Useful Resources

The Congressional Yellow Book Directory and *The Federal Yellow Book Directory*
> Leadership Directories, Inc.
> 1001 G St., NW, Suite 200 East
> Washington, DC 20001

Government Job Finder: Where the Jobs Are in Local, State, and Federal Government, by Daniel Lauber and Deborah Verlench, is a resource that contains hundred of sources for federal, state, and local government jobs. It also covers many government career options and describes dozens of sources of government job openings in Canada and overseas.

Moody's Municipal Manual and *Moody's Government Manual*
    Moody's Investors Service
    99 Church St.
    New York, NY 10007

Co-Op and Internship Programs

While in college, it is possible to test out engineering career options in federal, state, and local governments through participation in your university's cooperative engineering education (co-op) program. In addition, co-op is one of the best ways to secure a permanent engineering position with a government agency, because co-op allows you to alternate periods of paid work experience in an agency with periods of academic study. As a co-op student with a government agency, you might be considered an employee of the agency. Upon graduation, this might make it possible for you to convert your co-op employment to permanent employment without competition, if a full-time position is available. At the federal level, this conversion means that your seniority is dated from your original employment date as a co-op student. This has a positive impact on your eligibility for certain federal benefits, including sick leave, vacation, and ultimately retirement. See your co-op office about applying to federal agencies in which you are interested.

Special internship programs allow undergraduate engineers and entry-level engineers to experience employment opportunities at high levels of the federal government. There are two programs that engineering graduates should explore. The first is the Washington Internships for Students of Engineering (WISE) program (wise-intern.org). WISE is a unique summer internship program through which undergraduate engineering students learn how engineers contribute to public policy decisions on complex technological matters.

Participants are selected on the basis of academic performance and demonstrated leadership skills. WISE interns are exposed to a variety of public policy issues. Sponsorship of the WISE program rotates among several professional engineering associations rather than through a federal agency. Professional societies assume leadership of this program. The associations involved include:

American Association of Engineering Societies (aaes.org)
American Institute of Chemical Engineers (aiche.org)
American Nuclear Society (ans.org)
American Society of Heating, Refrigerating and Air-Conditioning
    Engineers (ashrae.org)
American Society of Mechanical Engineers International (asme.org)
ASTM International (astm.org)

Institute of Electrical and Electronics Engineers (ieee.org)
SAE International (sae.org)

In addition to jointly funding the internship with support of the National Science Foundation and the American Association of Engineering Societies, the sponsoring societies work with their WISE interns to select a research topic for the summer program.

If you are interested in this program, you should contact either the undergraduate studies office at your school of engineering or the professional association in your discipline to get more information.

The second program is the Presidential Management Intern (PMI) Program. PMI also seeks "the best and the brightest" for jobs in various areas of the federal government. Appointments are for two to three years. The technical track allows an engineering graduate to start as a GS-9. Initial appointments are usually handled by the graduate studies office at your school of engineering. Additional information can be obtained by writing to the Presidential Management Intern Program, OPM, Room 6336, 1900 E Street NW, Washington, DC 20415.

The benefits of both of these programs include high prestige and exposure to political and industry leaders. In addition, these programs provide a career track that prepares you for high-level positions in the federal system.

If your interests are more focused on the state or municipal level, the governor's office will help you identify special programs at the state level. You should also contact the mayor or city manager's office for opportunities at the local level.

If you have an interest in intelligence work, there are numerous government agencies that offer the opportunity to work with state-of-the-art technology. For full-time as well as co-op or internship positions, you must begin the application process early. Intelligence agencies can take up to twelve months to process your application and complete the security checks necessary for you to be employed. Because co-ops are considered employees of these agencies and interns can be placed in sensitive areas, they must also complete the entire application and security check process. Therefore, make sure your application is submitted well in advance of your desired starting date.

Possible Employers

As well as one of the largest employers of engineers, the federal government is consistently an important employer of women, minorities, and people with disabilities. Some federal agencies have a more impressive record of equal-opportunity hiring than some industries in the private sector. The following are agencies that you may want to investigate.

National Aeronautics and Space Administration (NASA) (nasa.gov, nasajobs.nasa.gov)
U.S. Army Corps of Engineers (usace.army.mil, usace.army.mil/working .html)
U.S. Department of Defense (defenselink.mil, defenselink.mil/other _info/careers.html)
U.S. Environmental Protection Agency (epa.gov, epa.gov/ezhire)
FBI Career Opportunities (fbi.gov, fbijobs.gov)
U.S. Food and Drug Administration (fda.gov, usajobs.opm.gov/a9fda .htm)
National Oceanic and Atmospheric Administration (NOAA) (noaa.gov, jobsearch.usajobs.opm.gov/a9noaa.asp)
Central Intelligence Agency (cia.gov, cia.gov/careers/index.html)
National Security Agency (nsa.gov, nsa.gov/careers)

The U.S. Department of Energy operates national laboratories (energy.gov /organization/labs-techcenters.htm) across the country. These labs and technical centers house world-class facilities where more than thirty thousand scientists and engineers perform cutting-edge research. These labs are:

• **Fermi National Accelerator Laboratory (FNAL or Fermilab) (fnal.gov):** Fermilab explores the fundamental nature of matter and energy by providing leadership and resources for qualified researchers to conduct basic research at the frontiers of high-energy physics. Located in Batavia, Illinois.

• **Lawrence Livermore National Laboratory (LLNL) (llnl.gov):** Science and technology for global security, global ecology, and bioscience. Laboratory employees work with industrial and academic partners to increase national economic competitiveness and improve science education. Located in Livermore, California.

• **Lawrence Berkeley National Laboratory (LBL) (lbl.gov):** LBL's research and development activities are designed to advance the frontiers of science in the areas of advanced materials, life sciences, energy efficiency, detectors, and accelerators. Located in Berkeley, California.

• **Brookhaven National Laboratory (BNL) (bnl.gov):** BNL creates and operates facilities for use by university, industrial, and government personnel in basic and applied research in the physical, biomedical, and environmental sciences, and in selected energy technologies. Located in Long Island, New York.

- **Oak Ridge National Laboratory (ORNL) (ornl.gov):** ORNL conducts basic and applied research and development to create scientific knowledge and technological solutions in key areas of science in order to increase the availability of clean, abundant energy; restore and protect the environment; and contribute to national security. Located in Oak Ridge, Tennessee.
- **Argonne National Laboratory (ANL) (anl.gov):** ANL conducts research in four broad categories: basic science, scientific facilities, energy resources, and environmental management, with programs ranging from studies of the atomic nucleus to global climate change research. Located at sites in Argonne, Illinois, and Idaho Falls, Idaho.
- **Sandia National Laboratories (SNL) (sandia.gov):** Designs all non-nuclear components for U.S. nuclear weapons, performs a variety of energy research and development projects, and works on assignments that respond to national security threats. Located at sites in Albuquerque, New Mexico, and Livermore, California.
- **National Renewable Energy Laboratory (NREL) (nrel.gov):** NREL promotes a sustainable energy future by developing renewable energy technologies, improving energy efficiency, advancing related science and engineering, and facilitating commercialization of these technologies by collaborating with industry. Located in Golden, Colorado.
- **Pacific Northwest National Laboratory (PNNL) (pnl.gov):** PNNL creates knowledge of natural, engineered, and social systems; solves legacy environmental problems; addresses environmental needs with technologies that prevent pollution; and lays the technical foundation for cleaner energy and industrial processes. Located in Richland, Washington.
- **Ames Laboratory (AMES) (ameslab.gov):** Works in materials research, high-performance computing, and environmental science and management to find solutions to energy-related problems through the exploration of physics, chemistry, engineering, applied mathematics, and materials sciences. Located in Ames, Iowa.
- **Los Alamos National Laboratory (LANL) (lanl.gov):** Research and development directed at enhancing the security of nuclear weapons and nuclear materials worldwide and managing the national nuclear stockpile. Located in Los Alamos, New Mexico.
- **Stanford Linear Accelerator Center (SLAC) (slac.stanford.edu):** SLAC examines the structure of atoms using x-rays and beams of electrons and positrons. These studies help to shed light on issues in the fields of

physics, biology, chemistry, medicine, and environmental science. Located in Menlo Park, California.

• **Princeton Plasma Physics Laboratory (PPPL) (pppl.gov):** PPPL is dedicated to developing the scientific understanding and key innovations that will lead to a fusion energy source, as well as to conducting research in plasma science and providing the highest quality of scientific education. Located in Princeton, New Jersey.

• **Idaho National Engineering and Environmental Laboratory (INEEL) (inel.gov):** INEEL comprises nine major applied engineering, interim storage, and research and development facilities. Located between Idaho Falls and Arco, Idaho.

• **Thomas Jefferson National Accelerator Facility (TJNAF or Jefferson Lab, formerly CEBAF) (jlab.org):** Jefferson Lab is a basic research laboratory built to probe the nucleus of the atom to learn more about the structure of matter. Located in Newport News, Virginia.

• **National Energy Technology Laboratory (NETL) (netl.doe.gov):** NETL addresses energy and environmental problems by researching, developing, and demonstrating technology in order to advance it into the commercial marketplace. Located at sites in Morgantown, West Virginia, and Pittsburgh, Pennsylvania.

• **Environmental Measurements Laboratory (EML) (eml.doe.gov):** EML provides program management, technical assistance, and data quality assurance for measurements of radiation and radioactivity relating to environmental restoration, global nuclear nonproliferation, and other priority issues. Located in New York, New York.

• **Bettis Atomic Power Laboratory (BAPL) (bettis.gov):** BAPL supports the development and use of advanced propulsion systems for U.S. Navy vessels by performing basic research; testing new components; and providing technical expertise during construction, maintenance, and refueling. BAPL headquarters is located in Burlington, Massachusetts.

• **New Brunswick Laboratory (NBL) (nbl.doe.gov):** NBL specializes in the measurement science of nuclear materials. The laboratory provides reference materials, measurement and measurement evaluation services, and technical expertise for evaluating measurement methods and safeguards measures in use at other facilities. Located in Argonne, Illinois.

• **Knolls Atomic Power Laboratory (KAPL) (kapl.gov):** KAPL supports the United States Naval Nuclear Propulsion Program by developing advanced propulsion technology, providing technical support for operating naval reactors, and providing training for naval personnel. Located in Niskayuna, New York.

Additional Agencies That Hire Engineers
Centers for Disease Control (cdc.gov)
Department of Transportation (dot.gov)
Department of Energy (doe.gov)
Department of Health and Human Services
    (hhs.gov)
Department of Agriculture (doa.gov)
Department of Commerce (doc.gov)
Department of the Interior (doi.gov)
Department of State (state.gov)
Federal Communications Commission
    (fcc.gov)
Housing and Urban Development (hud.gov)
Internal Revenue Service (irs.gov)
U.S. Forest Service (fs.fed.us)

Possible Job Titles

Some possible job titles that you may see in your pursuit of a government job opportunity include, but are not limited to:

Ceramicist
Computer-aided design engineer
Design engineer
Developmental engineer
FBI agent
Field services engineer
IRS agent
Materials engineer
Naval architect
Ordinance engineer
Quality assurance engineer
Reliability engineer
Research engineer
Safety engineer
Secret service agent
Systems engineer
Technical writer
Test engineer

Professional Associations

A number of associations address the specific needs and concerns of government employees. The organizations include:

American Federation of Government Employees
80 F St. NW
Washington, DC 20011
afge.org

American Federation of State, County, and Municipal Employees
1625 L St. NW
Washington, DC 20036
afscme.org

National Association of Government Employees
159 Burgin Pkwy.
Quincy, MA 02169
nage.com

9

Path 4: Education

With the increased demand for math and science teachers in middle schools and high schools, some undergraduate engineering students are deciding to take an extra year of study, at the undergraduate or graduate level, to become certified teachers. These students have usually fully assessed their personal values, strengths, and interests and determined that teaching at this level is a better fit for them than some of the more lucrative career paths available to bachelor-level engineers.

Most engineers take the required number of hours in math to become certified math teachers in most public school systems. In addition, depending on the engineering major, some can qualify for certification to teach physics, chemistry, or biology.

Engineering students do not always consider this career path because the pay differential with industry can be significant. However, for those who enjoy working with young people and are skilled in conveying subject matter with enthusiasm and knowledge, schoolteaching is a very satisfying and rewarding career.

Like Professional Engineering licensure, teacher certification requirements vary from state to state and by discipline. Therefore, it is advisable to check with the state in which you plan to teach or with a school or college of education in that state for assistance in reviewing your transcript to see what courses you will need to take for certification. Education programs that prepare people for certification are generally accredited by the National Council for the Accreditation of Teacher Education (NCATE). This association is also a good source of information on how to become a certified teacher of math and/or science.

More commonly, engineers who pursue graduate-level education and research in their specific field of engineering will find that college and university teaching is a viable career option. Faculty members in engineering not only enjoy and value learning, but also actively contribute to the body of knowledge associated with their field while preparing the next generation of engineers.

Some engineering faculty pursue research as the major emphasis in their faculty role. However, while research funding and publications may be of paramount importance in nearly every school of engineering, poor teaching is viewed negatively even at institutions that place primary emphasis on research.

Because the preparation of future engineers is vital to the profession and to the nation, teaching is at the center of any academic career. But while some schools of engineering emphasize research, others such as the Rose-Hulman Institute of Technology (rose-hulman.edu) place primary emphasis on teaching. Still others emphasize relationships with industry. Fairfield University's BEI School of Engineering (fairfield.edu/x837.html) employs practicing engineers as faculty in their part-time, evening, and weekend programs. The mission of this unique school of engineering is academic preparation that meets the needs of local industry and emphasizes practical applications.

Obviously these different institutional missions create different environments in which engineering faculty work. Nonetheless, an important aspect of an academic career for all engineering faculty is interaction with students, whether undergraduate or graduate students, and their academic colleagues. Engineering faculty enjoy a special fellowship and camaraderie among themselves and their students. This interaction usually transcends the campus to include faculty, students, and practicing engineers around the country and the world.

These scholarly interactions have meant that engineering faculty have always had a lead role in the pursuit of technological advances. Working hand-in-hand with government and industry, faculty research in engineering has advanced the knowledge base in every field. With the growing interest in maintaining our competitive advantage in the global marketplace and with technology increasingly becoming a part of our everyday life, the role of engineering faculty members has become even more significant.

Engineering faculty are at the center of the technology transfer that is taking place as defense-related technologies are transformed for industrial and consumer usages designed to improve our quality of life at home and at work. Through scholarly research, innovative teaching of engineering design, and major contributions to the literature of their field, engineering faculty have a significant impact on our national security and overall quality of life.

While teaching has always been considered a noble profession, engineering education takes on dimensions that few other disciplines can approach. Engineering faculty expect a high degree of ethical competence from their students by continually teaching the responsibilities and consequences of engineering decisions.

Definition of the Career Path

Teachers and faculty members have been such a constant and central part of your life for so many years that you might not have considered a career path in the teaching profession. It might be difficult to picture yourself in front of a college classroom or leading a research team as a faculty member at a major university. However, if you enjoy the process of learning and growing intellectually and if you like research and laboratory work, engineering education may be a very appropriate career path.

Where to Begin

An academic career does not begin with your first faculty appointment. It actually begins when you start to think about going to graduate school. In some instances, you might find that you are being advised to obtain experience in the field before pursuing a graduate degree. This advice is not contradictory. It is quite sound in today's academic environment. Industry experience, as an engineering co-op student or as a full-time employee, will provide an excellent foundation for an academic career. There are two major benefits to this approach.

First, as a future faculty member your industrial experience will give you a better understanding of the issues that face engineers engaged in professional practice. This is extremely important, as most of your students will pursue career paths in business, industry, or government. Your understanding of the issues and constraints they will face will be of significant value to them.

Second, practical engineering experience will help you focus more clearly on the objectives of your graduate study. It might even help you determine the subspecialties you wish to pursue and who would be the best faculty person to study with in that area.

Upon entering graduate school, your appointment as a graduate research assistant or a graduate teaching assistant can form the basis for a successful academic career. Prestigious fellowship awards to support your graduate education, such as the National Science Foundation Fellowship (nsfgradfellows.org), might also position you well for a faculty position after you complete your graduate studies.

Today it is almost a necessity to have postdoctoral research experience before receiving an appointment to an engineering faculty. A track record of successful research and scholarly publications provides important credentials when competing for faculty positions. Your postdoctoral time, usually at a university different from the one awarding your Ph.D., will provide you with additional time to build your scholarly reputation in the field.

Positions in Academia

Most engineering faculty begin in a postdoctoral position doing research with and working under the guidance of a senior faculty member at a school or college of engineering. When the postdoctoral experience ends (in one to three years), the next step is to seek an appointment as an assistant professor in a "tenure track" position. This is the point at which you become a full-fledged member of the faculty. Assistant professors on the tenure track have up to seven years to become tenured, but in reality they have six years to build their credentials for tenure. "Tenure cases" usually are presented to the promotion and tenure committees for review and approval during your sixth year of employment. If you are not granted tenure and promoted to the level of associate professor, you have the seventh year to seek positions outside of academia or at another institution.

In general, associate professors have achieved tenure and become permanent members of the engineering faculty. This status permits them to serve on certain policy committees and to review new faculty for tenure. It is fully expected that they will remain active in their teaching, research, and/or service to the profession. By doing so, they may qualify for promotion to full professor. This is usually the highest academic appointment that one can receive. However, for truly outstanding achievement in a specialized field of engineering, faculty can be appointed to "chaired" positions. This honor is bestowed on faculty by both the school of engineering and a major donor to the school who contributes the funding to support the salary and research of a chaired professor. This is a very select group among the faculty.

Once tenured, some faculty seek administrative responsibilities within their departments, the school, and/or the college or university. Some engineering faculty serve as chairpersons of their departments. In this capacity, they oversee admissions, curriculum development, faculty appointments, student affairs, departmental budgets, research agendas, and expenditures for classroom, laboratory, and office facilities for the faculty and students.

The dean of the school of engineering, as well as the associate and assistant deans, are usually engineering faculty. The dean provides leadership and has overall responsibility for the direction and integrity of the school. Deans usually delegate schoolwide responsibility for such areas as undergraduate education, graduate studies and research, administration, and external affairs to a team of assistant and associate deans, depending on the size of the school.

After service in administrative roles within the school of engineering, some faculty seek positions in the central administration of colleges and universities. Some rise to the position of university president. Other positions that engineering faculty tend to hold are provost or vice president for academic affairs, vice president for graduate studies and research, vice president or director for sponsored programs, director of technology transfer, and positions in government and industry relations on behalf of the college or university.

The career path from graduate assistant to university administrator can be exciting and challenging. But it requires long hours and real dedication. Engineering education is definitely not a nine-to-five job!

Working Conditions

The working conditions in colleges and universities differ widely. Each campus has its own unique personality and style. An important determinant of these differences is the mission of the overall institution and the focus of the school of engineering. The differences are also attributable to the individuals who make up the engineering faculty.

Every college and university catalog clearly states the institution's mission. Prospective faculty members should read those statements carefully. In addition, the school of engineering's own mission statement, if it has one, should be examined as well. These statements of purpose will tell you what activities the institution values and what activities it will reward.

Some institutions emphasize faculty research and publications. Faculty in these settings are expected to set a research agenda for themselves; secure outside funding from industry, foundations, and/or government agencies; publish their results; sponsor colloquia and symposiums; and become recognized experts in their specific area of engineering. Schools that are ranked among the top twenty-five graduate engineering programs in the country tend to fall into this category.

While classroom teaching takes special talent and training, a research-oriented institution will tolerate a slightly different level of teaching ability if the faculty member is a truly outstanding researcher. This type of university also values faculty activity in professional societies. All of these factors bring recognition and stature to the faculty member, the department, and the school.

Other schools of engineering emphasize teaching. In these settings, innovative teaching techniques and publication of engineering textbooks are expected. The faculty/student ratio is an important consideration because the academic development of the students is critical to the mission and goals of this type of institution. This is not to say that teaching is undervalued in research-oriented universities. All institutions of higher learning strive to provide a high level of teaching. However, at institutions that focus exclusively on teaching, faculty members are held more accountable for their expertise in the classroom, as opposed to research expertise.

In addition to teaching- and research-oriented institutions, there are also institutions whose mission it is to serve a specific industry, or industry in general. Universities such as the Embry-Riddle Aeronautical University (erau.edu) are excellent examples of engineering programs devoted to professional practice in a particular industry. These institutions value service to business, industry, and government.

There is a strong expectation at these schools that faculty will work to meet industry needs and to emphasize practical applications. Industry experience is a key factor in determining faculty rank and promotion. Faculty in these institutions will often also hold professional licensing in their engineering discipline.

No matter the educational environment in which you teach, you will probably feel that you have not had enough formal preparation in teaching methodology. If you do have the opportunity to serve as a graduate teaching assistant, you may have some basic experience. However, it is advisable for new engineering faculty to seek assistance from senior faculty in the department and at your degree-granting institution on how to improve their teaching techniques. Most colleges and universities now have centers for teaching excellence. Make use of these resources.

In the past, the ability to structure a class and fulfill a curriculum was based in part on the belief that new faculty will accomplish this in the same manner in which they mastered much of their own graduate study—through autonomous learning. This is not a good course of action to take. If you find yourself in the situation of having little actual classroom experience, ask for—demand, if necessary—guidance and assistance in mastering good teaching techniques. Your students deserve it. Don't jeopardize your chances for tenure, however, by ignoring your research and service obligations, if that is what your institution values!

Excellent teaching, research productivity, and professional service do not automatically mean that engineering faculty can continue to teach and do research at their institutions indefinitely. In most instances, faculty members, who are on the "tenure track" must be reviewed by a rigorous process at the end of their fifth year. While some institutions do not have, or have abolished, tenure, the majority still maintain this process of peer review to assure the quality of the faculty. At the end of the tenure process, faculty who are granted tenure are generally assured of a long-term commitment of employment with the college or university.

The Tenure Process

The concept of tenure was instituted to protect faculty members' rights to teach their subject matter without threat of losing their jobs if someone disagreed with their point of view. Higher education is built on the principle of critical thinking and open exchange of ideas. Tenure is part of the process that protects those aspects of higher learning.

In today's climate, tenure increasingly comes under attack for "guaranteeing a job for life." However, if you plan to pursue an academic career, you should know and understand the process in general and at your institution.

Promotion and tenure is taken very seriously on academic campuses. It is a time-consuming and thoughtful process. The candidates for tenure must prepare their "case." How this preparation occurs and what should be included is up to the institution. It is advisable to ask your department chairperson for the tenure and promotion criteria when you accept your initial appointment. Know the "rules of the road" before you start out on the journey!

Establish a filing system that reflects the set of criteria you are given. This keeps you organized and on-target for your institution. It is also a good idea to check every year to see if the rules have changed. Sometimes the process is reorganized or a new type of measure is added to the process. Administrative changes in department heads, deans, and presidents can result in significant shifts in the standards. You do not want to be surprised when it is your year to be reviewed for tenure.

It is also advisable to read the curricula vitae of tenured faculty in your department if these materials are publicly available. If it is obvious that your school tenures people with strong research and significant outside funding for research, do not make the mistake of thinking that outstanding teaching will substitute for that. It won't. Many people have been denied tenure because they pursued a career path different from the one the institution customarily values and rewards. Remember that untenured assistant professors do not change the academic system no matter how "right" their point may be!

Tenure cases are reviewed at the following levels: department, school, university, central administration, and the board of visitors or trustees. At the department level, a committee of tenured faculty review the "tenure file" that the candidate presents. The members of the committee vote to grant or deny tenure and then send their recommendation and the tenure file to the department chairperson.

The chairperson reviews the faculty committee's recommendation and the candidate's file and sends his or her recommendation to the school's Promotion and Tenure Committee (commonly referred to as the P&T Committee). If it has been recommended that tenure be denied, the department chairperson will usually notify the candidate. At that time, the candidate can decide to withdraw the case or have the file sent to the P&T Committee with the information from both the faculty committee and the department chairperson.

If the chairperson recommends that tenure be granted, the tenure file and the materials from the faculty committee and a letter from the department chairperson are then forwarded to the P&T Committee for the school of engineering. At this point, the P&T Committee, usually made up of tenured faculty from all departments in the school, reviews the entire file and the departmental recommendations. The committee votes and reports its vote and recommendation to the dean.

The dean follows the same procedures that the department chairperson followed. All review documents and the file are analyzed and the dean makes the school's recommendation to the institution-wide P&T Committee. This committee is generally made up of tenured faculty from all of the departments, schools, and colleges within the institution. They review all the documents and the file and vote to grant or deny tenure. The college or university P&T Committee report the recommendation to the provost or vice president for academic affairs.

At this level the case is reviewed again and a recommendation is made to the president. From there it is taken to the board of visitors or trustees for final action. In most cases the entire process takes one academic year to complete.

The Tenure File. In most schools, the tenure case is made up of the following components:

1. A curriculum vitae
2. A list as well as a complete set of your publications. Some institutions require copies of reviewer comments on publications recently submitted to referred journals.
3. Citation index
4. A statement of research accomplishments and goals
5. A statement of teaching accomplishments and goals and the following documentation: course outlines, course enrollment records, and descriptions of innovative teaching techniques or approaches
6. Teaching evaluations prepared by students, the department chairperson, and peer review visits to the classroom, if conducted at the institution
7. Letters of recommendation from leaders in your field. In some institutions, you can supply this list of names. In others, the list is either negotiated with the department chairperson or selected by the department chairperson without your input.

Tenure is a highly valued credential among engineering educators. It carries significant responsibility and allows the faculty member to pursue the challenges of teaching and research that are important to the individual and to the profession. It is the most significant condition for continuing an academic career path at most colleges and universities.

Education and Qualifications

When and how does one begin to qualify for faculty appointments in schools of engineering? Because most engineering faculty are hired for their advanced degrees and their scholarship in a specific area of their field, most hold a doctoral degree. This is particularly true for those who work at four-year colleges and universities.

Two-year technical schools may not require a doctoral degree, but they almost always require a master's degree in the appropriate engineering discipline. While there are always some exceptions, it is increasingly rare for a school of engineering to have faculty who do not hold advanced degrees.

If you are planning on a career in academia, your decision about which graduate school to attend is very important. You want to pursue your graduate study at an institution that will best prepare you for the type of teaching career that you are seeking.

A top-ranked institution provides the best platform for an academic career, so long as you can perform well and earn the support of your major professor. Graduate schools of engineering that are consistently ranked in the top twenty-five programs are excellent schools to consider. Their reputation, and your personal credentials, will help you compete for postdoctoral and faculty positions in the years to come.

There are several directories of graduate schools of engineering. The American Society for Engineering Education (asee.org) publishes the *Directory of Engineering Graduate Studies & Research*. The directory includes alphabetical and geographical indexes, as well as comparative tables of research expenditures, student enrollments, degrees awarded, and faculty appointments. There are full-page profiles of U.S. and Canadian universities and an index of engineering research subject areas.

A number of directories will provide information on such things as the faculty/student ratio (it should be low), the number of master's and doctoral degrees awarded annually, the percentage of women and minorities admitted, who to contact for application materials, and the list of standardized tests that are required.

Publications such as Gourman's (gourman.com) rate graduate and professional programs, both domestic and international. *U.S. News and World Report* (usnews.com/sections/education/index.html) annually ranks graduate schools and specific graduate programs. In addition, the National Academy of Science and Engineering (nationalacademies.org) publishes a rating of graduate programs periodically. All of these directories are useful tools when making a decision about which graduate engineering program to attend.

However, another source of information is often overlooked. The engineering faculty in your undergraduate program have a wealth of knowledge about their colleagues and other schools of engineering. Unfortunately, many people who plan to go on to graduate school never think to ask them for advice and guidance. This is particularly true when you are in the process of completing the graduate school application form.

Unlike admissions to undergraduate school, graduate applications are reviewed and evaluated by engineering faculty members in the department in which you plan to study. Before you apply to a graduate engineering program it is advisable that you talk with faculty in your undergraduate department and learn all that you can about the faculty in the department to which you plan to apply.

- Where are their degrees from?
- What are their areas of expertise?
- What books and articles have they published?
- Are their engineering interests similar to yours?

The following tips on how to assess if the graduate faculty's research interests are similar to yours may help.

- Read resources such as the *Directory of Engineering Graduate Studies & Research* and *Peterson's Guide*. They provide indexes of engineering research areas and surveys of professional society research publications and journals. These resources highlight the nature of research being carried on at different universities and the faculty members doing it.
- Conduct literature searches to find research papers written by the faculty members to become more familiar with the field.
- Visit the website of the department in which you are interested. These sites will describe their active areas of research. Follow up with letters or e-mail to the faculty members who are active researchers and ask them about their work. It is important for you to determine if their areas of interest match yours. You also want to assess whether you think you could work and study with them.
- Visit engineering schools and tour the department in which you are interested. This is the best means to evaluate any school or department. How do you feel when you are on the campus? In the department? Talking to the faculty? Talking to current graduate students?

Key issues in deciding where to apply for graduate study include:

- A good match between your research interests and the department's strengths
- The reputation of the department and/or the specialization in which you are interested
- The overall quality of the institution

Getting into an Engineering Graduate School

Like many graduate programs, schools of engineering require the Graduate Record Examination (GRE). You should take the GRE during your senior year of college even if you do not think that you will be going on to graduate school. The scores are good for five years, and having taken the exam keeps all of your options for the future open. It can be intimidating to take this exam when you have not been in school for several years!

The next step in the process is completing the graduate application, which includes:

- Completing an application form
- Submitting an official transcript
- Providing three letters of reference
- Writing a statement of purpose
- Requesting financial assistance

Paying for graduate school should not be a barrier to an academic career in engineering. If you have a strong record of academic achievement, you should be competitive for numerous fellowships and graduate assistantships. These not only pay your tuition and fees but also provide a monthly stipend for living expenses. Some of these sources include:

- **Teaching assistantships.** These provide stipends, and sometimes tuition waivers, to full-time graduate students for assisting a faculty member in teaching undergraduate classes.
- **Research assistantships.** These provide stipends, and sometimes tuition waivers, to full-time graduate students for assistance on a faculty research project.
- **Fellowships.** These provide money to full-time graduate students to cover the costs of tuition and living expenses and are not based on an obligation to assist in teaching or conducting research. Some fellowships are funded by the school, while others are available from outside sources such as the National Science Foundation (NSF) at nsf.gov. Fellowships represent an excellent credential when applying for postdoctoral positions and ultimately faculty positions because they are so competitive.

If these sources of funding do not seem available to you, there are student loans available to graduate students. The American Society for Engineering Education (asee.org) has been instrumental in partnering with various organizations and agencies to offer scholarships, fellowships, and internship opportunities for engineering students.

When seeking funding for your graduate education, you need to do your homework. Talk to faculty and graduate schools. Learn as much as you can about the process of competing for fellowships and assistantships. If you prejudge your own competitiveness, you may be making a costly mistake and incurring unnecessary debt!

It is important to have a good undergraduate record and evidence of a commitment to the field. This commitment can be in the form of paid, related work experience or volunteer experience. The faculty committee that reviews applications and makes recommendations for financial assistance needs to see that you can make a substantive contribution to the school's teaching and/or research.

Earnings

In comparison to entry-level offers made by industry and consulting firms to new bachelor's-level engineers, faculty salaries may appear to be low at the outset of an academic career. However, several factors need to be considered.

First, the base salary for most faculty positions reflects nine- or ten-month contracts, not twelve months of income. Summer teaching and/or research funding for the summer can considerably increase that base salary.

Second, as the faculty member establishes a reputation in his or her field, salaries can be augmented with lucrative consulting fees from business, industry, and government. At research institutions, outside funding of research projects not only pays the faculty member's summer wages but also supports graduate students and their research.

Third, in the publish-or-perish world of academia, royalties from books, software, and/or patents also contribute to the engineering faculty member's overall income. Likewise, engineering faculty can become involved in entrepreneurial activities which can spawn financially successful business ventures.

There are several good resources to use to compare faculty salaries. Each year *The Chronicle of Higher Education* (http://chronicle.com/free/v47/i32/2001index.php3#info) publishes an extensive breakdown of all faculty salaries by rank, discipline, and institution. More specifically, the American Association of Engineering Societies (AAES) (aaes.org) compiles annual salary information. These figures can help you make comparisons of salaries from year to year.

Each July, AAES publishes *Salaries of Engineers in Education*. This report contains median, quartile, decile, and mean salaries across eighteen experience brackets for engineering faculty, by academic rank, contract types, and type of institution. The most recent data on engineering faculty salaries can be obtained by writing AAES Publications Department, Suite 403, 1111 19th St. NW, Washington, DC 20036-3690.

Specific engineering groups also report salary information relevant to their membership. For example, consortia of engineering schools annually report the faculty salaries for their member institutions. Some professional societies in each engineering discipline also report salary information for faculty in that discipline. These are all excellent resources to contact when you begin to negotiate your salary with schools of engineering.

It is important not to forget the leave and vacation time that teaching faculty have. This is often overlooked as a real benefit. However, at research institutions, it is fully expected that faculty will use that time to devote their full attention to research and publications. While the vacation time may seem nice, a two- or three-month vacation from research and writing will not get you tenured!

Career Outlook

The predictions of shortages in qualified faculty in engineering make the career outlook in academia bright at the present time. Increases in federal and state funding of higher education and in technology research plus the growing population among college age students are some of the factors operating to increase the need for new faculty. However, when positions become available the competition is stiff. Candidates need to be flexible and well prepared. They must also have strong motivation and a high energy level because it is increasingly difficult to get tenured at a leading university today.

Strategy for Finding the Jobs

Acquiring a college or university teaching position in engineering nearly always demands that you have completed a postdoctoral experience at an institution other than where you received your degree and that you are willing to relocate again after the completion of your postdoctoral years.

Engineering education usually has limited openings at any one time, and postdoctoral experience, one-year untenured appointments, part-time teaching assignments, and/or adjunct faculty status at an institution is no guarantee of earning a full-time position at that institution. Most departments have budget lines dedicated to full-time, potentially tenured faculty. This means faculty who are hired in those budget lines are expected to become a permanent part of the faculty and earn tenure and promotion when they qualify. Consequently, although there may be schools at which you would enjoy teaching or areas of the country you would prefer, the supply and demand for college professors usually will require you to relocate several times before you achieve your goal of a tenure-track assistant professor position.

Identifying Opportunities

The Chronicle of Higher Education is a weekly national publication listing junior college, four-year college, and university teaching positions in every field. The alphabetical arrangement of job titles and the institutional advertisements should be checked carefully.

The *Chronicle* typically will post positions under "Engineering" as well as under the specific engineering discipline (e.g., "Civil Engineering," "Mechanical Engineering," "Biomedical Engineering"). In addition, universities will often run advertisements listing all of their faculty and administrative openings. These are not necessarily in a particular sequence or order so you need to read the entire classified section when you are involved in a serious job search. There is an added benefit to taking the time to study these classified ads. Because they are not exclusively lists of engineering openings, you can learn a lot about the institution and its current situation. Are there faculty openings as well as department chairperson openings? Is the dean's job being advertised? How about the president? All of this information is of importance to a newly hired faculty member.

For engineers who are seeking to teach at the community college level, www.ccollegejob.com is another resource that provides a listing of vacancies at all levels of the institution, including faculty positions.

Prism, the monthly publication of the American Society of Engineering Education (ASEE), contains a classified section exclusively devoted to engineering faculty positions. The job descriptions in this publication tend to carry more detail about the position and the qualifications than do listings in the *Chronicle*. The number of listings, however, may be smaller. Therefore, both publications should be used. *The Chronicle of Higher Education* and *Prism* are widely available on college campuses and in schools of engineering.

Another excellent source of college-level positions will be the faculty contacts you make as you pursue your advanced degree. There is a well-established network that becomes active when schools are seeking to fill a faculty position. A personal recommendation from a colleague or former teaching associate will be welcomed by faculty at the hiring institution. For this reason, it's important to ensure that your faculty mentors and colleagues are well aware of your teaching and research interests and geographic preferences so they can recommend you and move the process along if an opportunity presents itself.

Because more and more universities are seeking faculty with some industrial experience, your industry contacts will also be a valuable resource. Through various "relations-with-industry" programs, department chairpersons will sometimes contact industrial liaisons for leads on strong candidates for faculty positions. It is advisable to reestablish contacts you may have had through your cooperative education or other work experience.

Attend professional meetings and present papers. You need to see and be seen, and your research needs to be shared with the engineering community. In addition, interviews are often conducted in these settings. As a graduate student, many of these conferences are available to you at substantially reduced fees or no fee at all. You should take advantage of them for the professional content and the opportunity to meet representatives of departments at other institutions.

Resources for Finding Jobs in Education and Academia

The Chronicle of Higher Education is the premier resource on academic careers at colleges and universities. This weekly publication has an extensive website (http://chronicle.com/jobs) that provides career advice and job listings. The source specifically for engineers is http://chronicle.com/jobs/faculty _resources.htm#engineering.

Other resources include:

Academic Careers Online (academiccareers.com)
Academic Employment Network (academploy.com)
The Academic Position Network (apnjobs.com)
CCollegeJobs.com (www.ccollegejobs.com)
School Technology Career Center (eschoolnews.org)

Preparing the Curriculum Vitae

Upon completion of your Ph.D. program, you will most likely be looking for a postdoctoral position at another university in order to expand your research interests and expertise. This stepping-stone to a full-time faculty position will require a curriculum vitae (C.V.), not a résumé. What sets the C.V. apart from the usual résumé is the presentation of your research interests and experience. In addition, the C.V. includes information about your personal scholarship and any courses you taught as part of a graduate teaching assistantship. If you served as a graduate student representative on academic, administration, and/or student affairs committees, these experiences are also included. Your major faculty adviser is the best source of assistance in constructing your first C.V.

In assisting you, your adviser will become more aware of your past experiences and your unique strengths. This can be extremely helpful to you when your adviser talks to colleagues about your next career move. A helpful resource to use before meeting with your adviser about your C.V. is Acy L. Jackson and C. Kathleen Geckeis's *How to Prepare Your Curriculum Vitae*, published by VGM Career Books. The book provides worksheets which guide you through a step-by-step process to describe, in draft form, all of your pertinent experiences and to help shape and organize your C.V.

Preparing for the Campus Interview

When preparing to interview for a faculty position, prepare a one-minute, five-minute, and fifteen-minute summary of your interests and/or thesis work. You will be asked many questions about your scholarly interests and your research. The dean, the department chairperson, the faculty, and the students will all want to know what you will add to their faculty.

The seminar you conduct during the interview process will be crucial in determining if you will be hired. In preparing a seminar as part of your job interview, engineering faculty strongly recommend that you:

- Explain why your research is of scientific or technological interest.
- Exhibit clarity in your presentation, not the obscurity of your work.
- Present definite conclusions.

Make sure you know what you are talking about and that you know every nuance and entry on your handouts and overheads. Not knowing your own material can be deadly! However, if asked a question to which you do not know the answer, say that you do not know but that you will find out and get back to them. This is a much better solution than to be caught blustering on an issue you are not familiar with.

Landing the Job

Once you are in a tenure track position, never lose sight of the fact that the "tenure clock" is ticking. At the end of your fifth year you will be submitting your tenure file. That means that you have to establish your reputation in the field quickly. You must stay focused to be successful in the academic career field.

Remember to define a narrow area of research in which you have a strong interest and become the expert in that area. Begin submitting funding proposals and scholarly papers right away. Publish in well-respected journals and present your work at conferences. Make every effort to meet people in your field. Invite likely references in the tenure process to speak in your department. Their visits can provide you with an opportunity to demonstrate the outcomes of your work.

Find a few good colleagues with whom you can collaborate. Be cautious about too much collaborative research, however. It may become difficult for a peer review committee to know if you were the primary contributor, or a secondary contributor to the collaboration. These questions can harm you during the tenure process.

It is crucial that you do a good job when teaching. Students pay tuition to receive good academic preparation. However, if you are at a research institution, do not get carried away with your teaching role. No matter what you think or what you hear, teaching will not earn you tenure in this environment. If teaching is your strength, you should focus your job search on colleges and universities where teaching is the primary mission.

Although your faculty contract may talk of three-fold responsibilities—teaching, research, and service—faculty members do not get tenured based on service. There will be plenty of time for professional service after tenure is awarded. To keep your academic career on track, ask for departmental reviews even if they are not given as a matter of course. And be open to the feedback and advice that you receive.

Possible Employers

Nearly 350 colleges and universities offer at least one accredited bachelor's degree in engineering or engineering technology. More than 200 U.S. and Canadian universities have accredited graduate programs in engineering. All of these institutions are possible employers of engineering faculty.

In addition, some large industries, such as Motorola and Abbott Laboratories, have begun their own in-house education and training programs tailored for their own technology and their own engineering staff. These continuing education centers for professional engineers may offer other possible employment opportunities.

Recently, engineering consulting firms provide training services, as well as technological services, to their clients and are a source of employment opportunities for doctoral-level engineers who have a strong interest in teaching.

Possible Job Titles

The following are standard job titles on academic campuses. The list demonstrates the range of opportunities that exist for engineering educators:

Postdoctoral fellow

Adjunct professor

Research associate

Engineering lecturer

Assistant professor, tenure track or non-tenure track

Associate professor, tenure track or non-tenure track

Full professor, usually only tenured but very occasionally nontenured

Program director

Department chairperson

Assistant dean

Associate dean

Dean

Vice president of research, graduate studies, technology, information systems, facilities, etc.

Professional Associations

The primary professional association for engineering educators is the ASEE. ASEE addresses issues of importance to engineering education through its website asee.org, various divisions, conferences, and publications, including the *Journal of Engineering Education* and *Prism*.

The ASEE divisional memberships are comprehensive and include:

Aerospace

Architectural

Biological and Agricultural Engineering

Biomedical Engineering

Chemical Engineering

Civil Engineering

College Industry Partnerships

Community College Constituent Committee

Computers in Education

Construction Engineering Constituent Committee

Continuing Professional Development

Cooperative Education

Design Engineering Education

Educational Research and Methods

Electrical Engineering

Energy Conversion and Conservation

Engineering Acoustics & Vibration Constituent Committee
Engineering and Public Policy
Engineering Design Graphics
Engineering Economy
Engineering Libraries
Engineering Management
Engineering Technology
Environmental Engineering
Experimentation & Laboratory Oriented Studies
Freshman Programs Constituent Committee
Graduate Studies
Industrial
Information Systems
Instrumentation
International
Liberal Education
Manufacturing
Materials Engineering
Mathematics
Mechanical Engineering
Mechanics
Minorities in Engineering
New Engineering Educators Constituent Committee
Nuclear Engineering
Ocean and Marine Engineering
Physics
Women in Engineering

To obtain more information about ASEE and its divisions, contact:

American Society for Engineering Education (ASEE)
1818 N St. NW, Ste. 600
Washington, DC 20036
asee.org

National Council for Accreditation of Teacher Education (NCATE)
2010 Massachusetts Ave. NW
Washington, DC 20036-1023
ncate.org

10

Path 5:
The Internet

Contributions to this chapter were made by Dr. Thomas Moriarty, Norton Abbott Analysis, Ltd.

According to eMarketer.com, the money made by companies doing business on the Internet increased more than 25 percent from 2005 to 2006 and sales are expected to continue to increase in "the healthy double-digit range" through 2008. In addition, the number of Internet users has tripled since 2000. So, there is no doubt that business is going to continue to move to the Internet; therefore, the Internet will continue to be a career path for engineers and computer scientists in the twenty-first century.

The dot-com bust in 2000 resulted in many people losing their jobs. However, the Internet job market did not totally disappear, and, like other sectors of the economy, the availability of jobs in this area will rise and fall in cycles over and over again. But there will always be opportunities in this new sector of the job market, particularly for engineers and computer scientists with the required skills. To be successful in entering and advancing on this career path, it will be important to know what to look for and what to expect. This chapter will provide some of the basics and point you to additional resources, particularly online resources, which will help in your search for an Internet job that is the best fit for you.

Definition of the Career Path

Because the Internet career field is new and growing, many different kinds of opportunities are available. They depend on the nature of the company that is offering employment, and the differences are significant. The differences are largely factors of the e-commerce marketplace The following descriptions reflect some of the different situations you might encounter as you look for employment in the Internet sector.

Well-Established Company, Moving into a New Business Area

Here your employment is fairly standard, an entry-level salary with decent health and insurance benefits, possibly stock options in the parent company after you have been there awhile. If the new venture is successful, and you perform well, according to the parent company's standards, you can expect to ride the wave and have good long-term employment within the parent corporation, even if you decide to leave the new venture area. If the new venture is not successful, the parent company is likely to eliminate it and many of the employees. However, again, if you perform well according to the parent company's standards, you may have the opportunity to move to another part of the company and continue your career in an established business area.

When the new venture is successful, it reflects well on the parent company's bottom line, but probably will not change the nature of the company or cause a big increase in the company's stock price. Stock-option programs give you long-term incentives to stay with the company, but they are not usually spectacular, since the weight of the company and its stock performance probably rests with its established businesses. Profit-sharing programs give you short-term incentives, but again they are usually based on the overall company's performance so you can expect them to be dominated by the performance of the existing businesses.

Start-Up Company, Well Funded by Venture Capital

Employment in start-up companies that are well funded by venture capitalists often has some interesting wrinkles and dynamics because the venture capital investors are interested in just one thing—making a big profit quickly. Venture capital groups typically invest in a broad number of start-up companies, and they expect many of them to fail. This means that investor profits are obtained from a relatively small percentage of the efforts that do really well. Further, just breaking even, or sustaining profits of 10 to 20 percent, is not what these investors seek. The investors will quickly cut their losses if anything happens to reduce the start-up's potential for big profits, such as a product failing to perform as advertised, failure to meet a time commitment for development or sales, or a competitor emerging with an edge. This can also include such things as public opinion that this new type of business may not be as viable as was once thought, or a sector recession. The important thing to realize with a company that has venture capital investors is that the venture capitalists are in control, and they are successful because they exercise that control to their own advantage.

You will often find that in a venture capital–backed start-up, salaries are at or slightly below the industry averages, and benefit packages tend toward bare-bones levels. A very attractive part of the compensation package here, however, is the stock options that could have great value if the company is very successful and it goes public or is bought by a larger company at a premium price. Occasionally, significant bonuses are given for spectacular accomplishments that directly contribute to the immediate success of the company. Another attractive feature of this situation is the intensity of the participants in this kind of venture. It has its downsides—long hours, heroic deadlines, and frustrating constraints—but they can often be outweighed by the excitement of the pursuit of the holy grail, a product that is wildly successful.

If you are looking for stability and long-term employment, be careful of the venture capital–backed start-up. On the other hand, if you can afford the risk, this situation can be like a wild ride on a roller coaster, with the possibility of a grand prize at the end.

Start-Up Company with Limited Funding

Many Internet companies start with a small group of individuals (founders) who have a good idea and invest their own time and money in developing it. In many instances this can work for a while, but the usual case is to find an "angel"—sometimes in the group, but more often outside the founding group—that can fund the start-up in the very early stages. The "angel" usually provides money for equipment and supplies, along with enough money for the group to live on as necessary, and in turn gets a share of ownership in the concept being developed. These very young start-ups are usually focused on proving the viability of their concept, and are working toward an actual demonstration.

Once the concept has been demonstrated, and maybe improved a bit from its original version, the next step is to try to make a business out of it. Things sometimes get a bit dicey at this stage, because the founders sometimes do not have the background in marketing, finance, manufacturing, sales, and so on that it takes to put it all together. Thus, the company often gets bigger and becomes more expensive to hold together. If there is enough money, the company presses on and tries to get its product into the marketplace. Alternatively, the company puts together a business plan and then shops the venture capital groups to find investors, and that tale is told in the preceding section.

As the company grows, the founders end up owning a smaller share of a much larger entity, and if you look at the worth of each founder's share, it generally grows considerably in this process. To the founders, this is a wild ride with downside risk, since they often have invested their own money and time in the enterprise. As founders of a successful enterprise, however, the prize at the end of the ride would be a significant share of a successful company, potentially worth millions.

Established Company in a Volatile Market

This situation is probably the most stable of all, since an established company already in the market should know what it is doing and already has a good market share, otherwise it wouldn't be there. Here, you can expect good salaries and benefits because these employers are competing with the start-ups but don't have the upside potential to offer through stock and options that the start-ups do. These companies keep their people through good salaries, benefits, working conditions, and profit sharing, but there isn't the huge rags-to-riches potential. The risks in this situation come from the market itself, and the volatility can be due to consumer demand changing and/or new technology being introduced that change the competitive playing field. Whatever causes market volatility, it still can have a profound effect on your life as it can cause layoffs, changes in product direction, and outsourcing, all of which can significantly affect your career with the organization.

Where to Begin

For those ready and able to take the Internet roller coaster ride, a good starting point is to determine the type of Internet organization for which you would like to work. Considering the self-assessment that you conducted in the first part of this book, it may be possible for you to decide which of the four types of organizations that we have described best matches your needs, values, and interests.

- Well-established company, moving into a new business area
- Start-up company, well funded by venture capital
- Start-up company with limited funding
- Established company in a volatile market

For example, if you are willing to take significant risks, the potential payoff of a start-up company with limited funding may hold the challenge that you are seeking. On the other hand, if you are not comfortable with that much risk, you may find Internet opportunities with more established organizations a better fit for you.

Even if you are not sure which of these options is best for you, or which will be available to you, it is still important to know what type of positions you are qualified to fill within any Internet organization. What are the skills that you most like to use? Do you like the challenges of working with SQL, PHP, or JavaScript? What about ColdFusion, HTML, Dreamweaver, or Macromedia Fireworks? These are a few of the skills that Internet employers might be looking for, but because technology changes so rapidly, there will probably be other skills that you will want and need to develop to stay up to date. It's advisable to check with your faculty and with websites like International Webmaster Association (www.iwanet.org) about the current skills required in the field.

Locating a specific Internet-related position within an organization can be challenging, if that organization is not an Internet company. The Net Economy is still young, and there tends to be a real lack of conformity in job titles from company to company. It is not uncommon for positions with similar responsibilities to have different job titles.

To help you better refine your search and to more clearly articulate how your skills can best be put to use, the following are descriptions of typical Internet positions and the tasks associated with them:

- Programmers write, test, and maintain the software necessary for computers to perform their functions.
- Computer engineers test and evaluate computer hardware and related equipment to assure compatibility with software programs and systems.
- Software engineers/software developers design, develop, and modify software programs to meet the needs of the e-business and the end-users.
- Systems analysts study data-processing problems and design new flows of information, and connect hardware and software to provide maximum benefit to the company and end-user.
- Network systems engineers or data communications analysts design and evaluate interfaces between network systems and computers or communications equipment, using modeling, analysis, and planning.
- Database administrators set up, test, change, and organize computer databases, using database management systems software.
- Network administrators design, test, and evaluate local area networks (LANs), wide area networks (WANs), the Internet, and other data communications systems.

- Computer and information systems managers plan, coordinate, and direct the computer-related activities of an e-business.
- Supply chain experts improve the efficiency, quality, and cost of linking vendors, distribution networks, manufacturing processes, and procurement activities so that inventory management results in higher-quality service to customers and lower operating cost to the e-business.
- Industrial engineers improve e-business processes so that new products and Web features can be added, and/or increased amounts of data about sales and customers can be analyzed.
- Computer/technical support specialists provide assistance, support, and advice to customers and users by troubleshooting and interpreting problems encountered with hardware, software, and systems.
- Graphic designers develop print and electronic designs and signage for websites, advertisements, and publications.
- Webmaster keeps the Web server running.

Other Job Titles
Writers and editors
Advertising sales agents
Product managers

John Kador (jkador.com/netjobs), author of *Internet Jobs!* categorizes the career paths of the Net Economy into three basic areas:

1. Content development
2. Infrastructure/hardware
3. Business/operations

Webfeet.com categorizes Internet employers as:

- **Publishers.** Online publications that make money selling advertising and subscriptions. Examples are leading newspapers and magazines.
- **Vendors.** Online merchants that sell goods and services online. Amazon.com is a good example.
- **Aggregators and portals.** Search engines and sites that serve as "home base" for people accessing the Internet.
- **Communities.** Sites where people can find others with common interests. Facebook and MySpace are good examples.

- **Consulting and support.** Companies that provide support and services to the Internet, such as AT&T and Comcast.

These categorizations can help identify and define the types of positions for which you would like to apply because there are opportunities for engineers and computer scientists in all of these areas.

In the *content development area*, the need is for people who are interested in and proficient at writing software programs and/or designing Web page content. In the *infrastructure/hardware area*, the need is for people who are interested in and proficient at developing hardware, building networks, maintaining network security, and serving as Webmaster. In the *business/operations area*, the need is for people who are interested in and proficient at marketing, public relations, and financial management. Engineers or computer scientists who have taken elective course work in one or more of these business areas can bring strong technological knowledge and good business awareness to the job. This combination will increase career options in the Net Economy as one's career unfolds. Consider that Amazon.com, one of the most recognized corporate names of the Internet career path, states that "intelligence, initiative, and big-picture thinking gets noticed." Similarly, Priceline.com says that their "network operations are responsible for the planning, engineering, installing, and full 24/7 production support of Priceline.com's Web service" and that "the Network Operations Team plays a critical role in company's day to day success." The more ways in which you can contribute will keep career opportunities on the Internet career path interesting, varied, and challenging.

Positions in the Internet Career Path

At the beginning, many loosely configured technology teams built the first-generation of e-commerce and e-business platforms. From these platforms new Internet companies and services continue to be launched. The strength and flexibility of the first-generation platforms have allowed for future growth and development of the current generation of business and commerce over the Internet.

Software engineers, database administrators, Web developers, network engineers, industrial engineers, and supply chain experts are all members of the new teams that are driving the evolution of e-commerce and e-business. Knowing some of the job titles or functions in which they work will help you define your own search.

Kador's categorization can be used to decipher some of the many types of Internet job titles. This information can be used to develop a list of keywords that can be used to search the Internet effectively for positions that most closely match your interests and skills.

Kador's Internet Job Categorization	Sample Entry-Level Job Titles
Content Development Jobs	Programmers
	• Application programmer
	• Systems programmer
	• Maintenance programmer
	• Object-oriented programmer
	• Software engineer
	Web developer
	Graphic designer
	Computer-based graphic designer
	Digital video-sound editor
Hardware/Infrastructure Jobs	Technical support
	• Webmaster
	• Intranetmaster
	Development
	• Program developer
	• Systems analyst
	• Junior UNIX administrator
	Operations
	• Computer operator
	Networking
	• Network support
	• Internetwork engineering
	Database
	• Database designer
	IT administration
	• PC support
	• Computer security
	• Data security
	• Cross-platform security
	• SAP security
	Testing and maintenance
	• Quality assurance
	• Software testing

Kador's Internet Job Categorization	Sample Entry-Level Job Titles
Business/Operations	Supply chain
	Industrial engineer
	Account development
	Advertising
	Public relations
	Corporate finance
	Product manager
	Strategic marketing
	Internal business consultant
	Media integration
	Internet sales engineer
	Presales support
	Net instructor

While you will need to come to the industry with up-to-date technical skills and knowledge in one or more of these areas, you will constantly acquire new skills and knowledge from continued training and education and from bright, hardworking, and committed colleagues. This new knowledge, coupled with increasing levels of experience in the Internet sector, can result in personal and professional satisfaction and success.

Other Job Titles
Network engineer
Network optimization engineer
Network tools and analysis engineer
UNIX system engineer
Software engineer
Software development engineer
Systems operator
Data mining analyst
Supply chain analyst
Industrial engineer
Product manager

Working Conditions

The rapid growth of the Internet sector has had a dramatic impact on the working conditions and the culture of the companies and/or divisions in which this enterprise is pursued. It is creative and talented people who are driving the Net Economy. Their knowledge and commitment are the equivalent of the raw materials and transportation systems that drive the industrial economy.

The commitment and intensity to develop and implement technological advances quickly and in a user-friendly manner is not a luxury. It is a necessity in maintaining the competitive edge to assure the company's continued viability. That is why some of the traditional ways of working do not hold true in the Internet industry. For example, Internet organizations typically have flattened organizational charts. They also tend to have a team-oriented approach to work. Interestingly, the team concepts are often maintained even though telecommuting is much more common in the Internet industry than in others.

While dress and decor may be casual, the intensity of the work and the immediacy of solutions and deadlines are the hallmark of this new career path. "Just-in-time," "real-time," and "365/24/7" expectations and needs place a higher and higher premium on accessibility, accuracy, agility, and commitment to solving organizational and customer problems. These factors can make Internet organizations exciting and intense places in which to work and learn.

Continuous education and training are also necessary to keep up with the changing landscape of the Web. Learning occurs in all manners in this environment, including distance learning opportunities, workshops, academic courses, and interaction with colleagues. For people with high levels of energy, a desire for ever-changing challenges and an intense work environment, and a love of learning, the Internet sector offers many rewarding opportunities—so long as they can tolerate significant levels of ambiguity and risk in this new frontier!

Education and Qualifications

Some very high-profile people in the Net Economy never obtained a bachelor's degree, but this is extremely uncommon! One only has to look at the geographic locations of the major "silicon hot spots" to recognize that they are positioned close to major clusters of institutions of higher education. A bachelor's degree is the minimum qualification for most positions, and highly developed technical skills are a must.

Because of the technological advances in both computer hardware and software, the basic entry-level skills will change rapidly every twelve to eighteen months. Continuing education and training is an absolute must to maintain a competitive edge in this career path. It is advisable to stay abreast of the changing technological needs of Internet organizations by looking at posted job descriptions and reading trade publications in your specific area of interest on a regular basis.

In the summer of 2001, the following samples of job postings all required a minimum of a bachelor's degree. In addition, the specifications for these positions illustrated the breadth and depth of the technological knowledge necessary to qualify for an entry-level position at some of the largest Internet employers of the time.

Software Development Engineer. Must be proficient in ANSI C, or demonstrable skill in some other language; experience with branching in CVS, Perforce, Subversion, or similar tools; Prefer proficiency in: Linux kernel configuration and building experience; Networking (Ethernet, TCP-IP, UDP, HTTP, RTP/RTSP, UPnP); Audio formats such as MPEG-1 L1,2,3, PCM/WAV, WMA, AC3, AAC; Video formats such as H.264, DiVX, Xvid, 3ivx, MPEG-1, MPEG-2, WMV; Demuxing and simple manipulation of these formats and experience incorporating partner code and debugging combined systems. Media Player, Playback Manager, Filter Architecture. or experience with C/C11 and Perl scripting languages; software development on Windows and Linux platforms; strong knowledge in design patterns, UML Modeling, and object-oriented design and implementation; in-depth knowledge of operating systems, particularly Linux, in such areas as threading, inter-process communications, TCP/UDP/IP, performance fine-tuning and tools, GUI; software porting and migration knowledge (Windows* to Linux* experience) a plus. Knowledge of any of the following telecom applications and protocol stacks is also a plus:

- Media Processing Functionality (play/record, tone detection/generation, audio conferencing, T.30 Fax)
- VOIP* / FOIP* systems and associated protocols/standards (Data transport over RTP/UDP, RTCP, RFC2833, RFC2198, T.38)
- Video Standards (H.261, H.263, H.264, MPEG4), Video Streaming and associated control, Audio/Video Synchronization

Database Development. Experience creating SQL-based data exports and reports; PL/SQL packages for data integration (import, cleansing, ETL); UNIX and scripting languages and authoring scripts (in Python) to automate data

continued

management tasks. Experience with Microsoft Reporting Services a plus or expert PHP and JavaScript skills, Python is a plus; Java experience would be ideal. Strong scripting and database skills, including Perl/CGI, MySQL, and JavaScript. Experience in a Unix/Linux and Apache environments as well as experience with SQL/MySQL, Oracle, and logical database design.

Quality Assurance Engineer. Experience with QA processes and testing website applications required; experience with scripting languages, Perl, Java, JavaScript required. Experience with XML, HTML, SQL, and Linux highly desired or Software Quality Assurance . . . create and write test plans and test scripts; testing XML; Web Services and WSDL testing. Experience with writing automated scripts and test tools (Unix Shell/Perl/Batch Scripting); SQL and data retrieval from a relational database: SQL Server, Oracle, etc.; Experience with Unix, especially Solaris and Linux, defect tracking systems and other software life cycle management tools (Bugzilla); SoapTest, SoapUI, JMeter, and J-Unit Web services tools and different SOAP clients (Java, PHP, Perl, .Net, C#) are preferred. Familiarity with quality methodologies such as: CMM, ISO, or IEEE is a plus.

Earnings

Because the Net Economy is new, it can be challenging to find reliable salary information about Internet jobs. While there are numerous websites that provide salary data, the diverse nature of Internet employers means that types and levels of compensation can vary widely. Some small start-ups may substitute stock options for regular salaries and some large corporations pay salaries in line with their regular compensation packages for engineers and computer scientists. If you are contemplating a position in the Internet sector, Dave Bracken, who writes for WetFeet.com (wetfeet.com/asp/article.asp ?aid=82&atype=Internet), recommends that you use some of the following websites as tools for setting your own salary expectations and assessing offers received.

The Wall Street Journal Careers (careerjournal.com/salaryhiring)
ZDNet's SalaryZone
    (http://search.zdnet.com/index.php?q=salary+survey)
Dice.com (http://dice.com)

Real Rates (realrates.com)
DataMasters (datamasters.com)
Webmonkey (webmonkey.com)

Career Outlook

The Internet is here to stay! That means that new ways of doing business have been, and will continue to be found. There will be jobs for industrial engineers to improve processes and supply chains. There will be roles for electrical and computer engineers to design faster and easier access to the Internet with innovations in computer hardware and wireless devices. Likewise, there will be roles for computer scientists to design new software applications, interfaces, and database programs.

The Internet is also changing how traditional engineering gets done. As engineers from around the world collaborate on design and production issues, the Internet is expected to expand more rapidly in business-to-business functions. The fact that the Internet can be used to get products and services directly to vendors, customers, and suppliers more efficiently means that it will require the expertise of engineers from every discipline in order to customize operations for a wide variety of engineering and manufacturing functions.

As the Internet industry moves to the next generation, some of the challenges that it faces include scaling, demand forecasting, increased personalization, and digital media. These challenges, and many others, keep the engineering teams engaged and excited about their impact on a new and expanding industry. Amazon.com asks "Are you interested in equations like finding the best intersection of features vs. performance? Are you interested in the complexities that come with offering millions of unique products, from thousands of suppliers, to tens of millions of customers, around the world, each with their own currencies and levels of customer sophistication?" These are some of the challenges that Amazon.com is facing. That is why companies like Amazon.com depend heavily on their ability to attract top engineering and computer science graduates who possess the necessary technical skills.

All of these facts make the Internet the fastest-growing sector of the economy. It is expected that increasing numbers of engineers and computer scientists will build their careers in the Internet sector. As noted above, the Internet has already been equated with the Industrial Revolution that marked the beginning of the twentieth century. The new and exciting career opportunities that resulted when society moved from an agrarian society to an industrial one are expected to occur again as we move from an industrial society to an Internet society. Jobs that do not exist today are expected to become the norm in the next ten to fifteen years. For those who are well prepared and those who stay prepared for this fast-changing sector of the economy, new and creative career paths will surely await.

Strategy for Finding the Jobs

In the article "How to Build Your Online Career," Judy DeMocker recommends the following strategies for finding an Internet job:

- Build a personal website to show your Web development skills.
- Create electronic versions of your résumé (you will need more than one version!).
- Research the companies in which you are interested.
- Join online discussion groups to build your knowledge of the field.
- Work on your personal communication skills—teamwork requires them!
- Continue your computer education at all times and at any level needed.
- Attend events such as job fairs and professional association meetings.
- Find an internship or co-op position with the kind of company for which you would like to ultimately work.
- Follow your dream. Keep your skills up-to-date and be sure that you enjoy the pace and ambiguity of this career path.

As in any career path, a successful job search strategy depends on a good understanding of the expectations of Internet employers. Here are eleven important expectations to keep in mind when planning your job search strategies:

1. Make rapid response to opportunities by having electronic cover letters and ASCII versions of your résumés, or URLs to your résumé on the Web—do not use attachments.
2. Be sure that the contact information (name, address, phone, e-mail) and URLs on your résumé are complete and accurate.
3. Test all versions of your résumé on various browsers, or make conditional HTML files of your résumé so that it is available to different browsers.

4. Always have hard copies of your résumé available upon request.
5. Target cover letters and résumés for each position for which you apply.
6. Organize one version of your résumé around your work experience and others around how your skills relate to Kador's content development jobs, infrastructure/hardware jobs, and/or business/operations jobs.
7. Use URL links only to your approved and most significant projects. Select projects that demonstrate the highest quality and complexity of your work and that have been approved by the sponsoring organization of the project. Do not violate any confidentiality agreements to which you and/or your school have agreed. Always check with your faculty and your employers or sponsors.
8. Become knowledgeable about the entire websites of organizations in which you are interested—not just the career page!
9. Use blogs and e-mail discussion lists but be sure to make your inquiries specific and informative, follow basic business etiquette, and be prepared to contribute back to the discussion lists.
10. Be sure to post your résumé only to the employer that responded to you when responding to e-mail list inquiries from employers. Do not post it to the entire e-mail list.
11. Be prepared for telephone screening interviews when applying for jobs online, and have your work samples organized and ready to take to one-on-one or site interviews.

The primary strategy for your Internet job search is the Internet! Learning the process and etiquette of Internet job searches is very important to your success in landing the job that you want.

Keep in mind that dot-com companies almost exclusively use the computer to manage recruitment and hiring. As a result, the electronic versions (yes, that was plural!) of your cover letter and your résumé must not only be well prepared in terms of content, they must be presented in a manner that maximizes the chances that they will be read, considered, and acted upon by the hiring organization.

WetFeet.com provides additional advice on techniques for submitting your résumé to dot-com employers. The advice includes suggestions such as making sure that your résumé is included in the text of your e-mail instead of sending it as an attachment. Because human resources professionals and recruiters receive so many e-mails and are very concerned about introducing the viruses that can come on attachments, they usually do not open attachments.

Tips on How to Land a Job in the Internet Industry

In addition to having strong cover letters and electronic résumés and being well prepared to interview, it is always advisable to maximize your chance of securing the ideal job by looking for it in areas of the country where the jobs will tend to exist. Although the landscape of the Net Economy changes rapidly and today's hot spots may become tomorrow's challenges, it is still advisable to know where any industry tends to group. For example, petroleum engineers increase their job prospects by seeking employment in Texas or in other Gulf states, in comparison to conducting a job search in Idaho. Likewise, automotive engineers increase their prospects by conducting their job search in Michigan rather than in Nevada. This is not to say that petroleum and automotive engineers do not work outside these certain regions, but finding a job can be made much easier when you are aware of where many opportunities may be located. This same principle applies to your search for Internet jobs.

To maximize opportunities, you may wish to target one or more of the top ten tech centers in the United States:

1. San Jose, California (Silicon Valley)
2. Dallas, Texas (Telecom Corridor)
3. Los Angeles/Long Beach, California
4. Boston, Massachusetts (Route 128 Corridor)
5. Seattle/Belleview/Everett, Washington
6. Washington, D.C./Northern Virginia (Silicon Dominion)
7. Albuquerque, New Mexico
8. Chicago, Illinois (Silicon Prairies)
9. New York, New York (Silicon Alley)
10. Atlanta, Georgia

Other growing high-tech hot spots are:

1. Phoenix/Mesa, Arizona
2. Boise, Idaho
3. San Antonio, Texas
4. Boulder, Colorado
5. Research Triangle, North Carolina

Keep in mind that this does not mean that Internet jobs do not exist outside of these areas or that you should look exclusively in these areas. New opportunities are presenting themselves every day, particularly as more and more cities and municipalities seek to attract Internet-oriented business. However, the areas listed above already have large numbers of Internet organizations, and it is reported that there are thousands of unfilled Internet positions in these regions of the country.

Suggested Reference Materials

Career Opportunities in the Internet, Video Games, and Multimedia, Allan Taylor, James Robert Parish, and Dan Fiden

Careers in Internet Consulting: The WetFeet.com Insider Guide, WetFeet.com, Steve Pollock, Gary Alpert

Careers in E-Commerce Software Development, Jason T. Roff and Kimberly A. Roff

Careers with Internet Service Providers, Deborah J. Miller

About.com's Guides to Graphic Design, Mary Beth and Paul Trautwein

About.com's Web Design Guide, Jennifer Kyrnin

Internet Jobs!, John Kador

Possible Employers

Increasingly, Internet career paths exist in large, well-established companies, as well as the small, entrepreneurial start-ups.

Some of the most established companies of the "Old Economy" now have a significant presence on the Internet. This means that there are increasing numbers of opportunities with established companies to pursue the Internet career path. Some of these include:

GE (gecareers.com)
Orbitz (orbitz.com/App/Careers)
Microsoft (microsoft.com/jobs)
Google (google.com/intl/en/jobs)
AT&T (att.com/gen/careers?pid=1)
Tellabs (tellabs.com/careers)
The Charles Schwab Corporation (http://jobs.schwab.com)
Time Warner (timewarner.com/corp/careers/index.html)
The Walt Disney Company (http://corporate.disney.go.com/careers/index.html)

Some of the Net Economy companies that continue to offer opportunities for engineers and computer scientists seeking to pursue the Internet career path are:

Amazon.com (amazon.com/jobs)
Priceline.com (priceline.com/jobs)
EBay (ebaycareers.com)
PayPal (paypal.com/cgi-bin/webscr?cmd=p/gen/
    jobs-outside)
Intuit (intuit.com/careers)
Yahoo! (http://join.yahoo.com)
HealthCentral (healthcenter.com/careers.html)
Morgan Stanley (morganstanley.com/about/careers/index.html)
Macrovision (macrovision.com/company/careers/index.shtml)

Related Occupations

As more and more people begin to use the Internet, new positions have begun to develop. John Kador identifies several in his book *Internet Jobs!* Among the new job titles that are emerging are:

- **Internet researcher:** This person searches the Internet for data, information, and people for clients such as lawyers, doctors, scientific researchers, writers, or recruiters.
- **Sensory interface developer:** This person finds ways to eliminate the frustrations that people experience with computers by developing new interfaces that provide the user with more efficient and effective information or services.
- **E-business evangelist:** This person works within an organization or with external clients to demonstrate the benefit of moving operations and function to the Web.
- **Subject matter mentor:** This person provides content and infrastructure for organizations to deliver customized training and education to their employers or clients.

In addition, as more companies see the need to move all or part of their operations to the Internet, new opportunities are developing for Internet consultants. Internet consultants bring expertise and corporate knowledge that help their clients perform business functions and compete on the Internet.

Internet consulting is a relatively new option for job seekers. Some potential employers in this area are:

Agency.com (agency.com)
Primavera (primavera.com/careers)
BearingPoint Management & Technology Consultants (bearingpoint
.com)
Organic, Inc. (organic.com)
PricewaterhouseCoopers (pwcglobal.com)
Viant (viant.com)
Sapient (sapient.com)

Professional Associations

Internet Professional Association
Limited
iBay, Level 10, Cyberport 2,
100 Cyberport Road, Hong Kong
iproa.org

HTML Writers Guild
119 E. Union St., Suite F
Pasadena, CA 91103
hwg.org

International Webmasters Association
119 E. Union St., Ste. E
Pasadena, CA 91103
iwanet.org

U.S. Internet Industry Association
1800 Diagonal Rd., Suite 600
Alexandria, VA 22314
usiia.org

The World Organization of Webmasters
9580 Oak Ave. Parkway
Folsom, CA 95630
E-mail: info@joinwow.org

Society of Internet Professionals
53 Mandel Crescent
Richmond Hill, ON
L4C 9Z1 CANADA
sipgroup.org

Usability Professionals' Association
140 N. Bloomingdale Rd.
Bloomingdale, IL 60108-1017
upassoc.org

Path 6:
Nontechnical Areas

A number of engineering majors decide that they would rather not to be "hands-on" engineers. For these individuals an engineering education provides an intellectual challenge for their strong aptitude for math and science. They do extremely well in the engineering curriculum but they do not want to be engineers.

These engineering majors tend to enjoy the applied aspect of engineering but they do not have an interest in the day-to-day work of a professional engineer. Fortunately, as more aspects of everyday life become technologically based, their engineering skills and expertise have become increasingly important to other fields. With the disciplined foundation of an engineering education, these individuals are able to enjoy careers outside of engineering.

These students' technical expertise is an asset in bridging the information gap between the engineering and the nonengineering worlds. Their quantitative skills are applicable in a variety of occupational areas. Their problem-solving skills and creativity are advantages in a growing number of fields such as medicine, law, finance, and journalism. Engineers often are able to bring a level of knowledge and understanding that would be very difficult, if not impossible, for a nonengineer to contribute. Because of the rigors of their academic preparation, they are attractive candidates for positions in many nonengineering fields.

Technical Writing

Technical writing is one of the growing fields in which engineers have many opportunities to apply their knowledge and skill. Today, technical writers are engaged in producing materials for a wide range of audiences from highly sophisticated, technical readers to the general public. In addition to covering scientific developments for trade publications and the popular press, technical writers also produce operating manuals, technical reports, contract proposals, and promotional brochures.

An example of this type of position for an electrical engineer would be a technical writer as described by Lockheed Martin:

Write technical documents supporting systems and project lifecycle including: Program and Project Management, Security, Configuration, Disaster Recovery Standard Operating Procedures (SOPs), Server Operations SOPs, Network SOPs, and Technology. Must have knowledge of and experience with CMMi processes and ISO and IEEE Standards. Proven ability to write technical documents such as procedure manuals, service manuals, and related technical publications concerned with installation, operation, and maintenance of electronic, electrical, mechanical, and other equipment as well as operational specifications, bulletins, articles, and marketing publications in clear and concise language. Able to acquire or verify knowledge of subject by interviewing workers engaged in developing products and services; observing performance of experiments and methods of production; referring to blueprints, sketches, engineering drawings and notes, trade and engineering journals, rewrites of articles, bulletins, manuals, or similar publications.

Within the broad field of technical writing, engineers also work as industrial publicists. Industrial publicists usually work in technical industries that need to communicate their products and services to technical consumers and the general public. In this capacity, the industrial publicist interacts with all types of media on behalf of their industry.

The day-to-day tasks of this professional can include everything from arranging on-camera interviews with technical experts to writing press releases explaining new technological breakthroughs. Being able to establish and maintain a network of contacts, in the media and outside of it, is a very important characteristic of these individuals. While the actual writing may be done in some degree of isolation, engineers in this field have to be comfortable interacting with a wide variety of people.

The work of the industrial publicist is becoming increasingly important. These professionals generate millions of dollars in publicity for their organizations. In recent years this has become a growing field of employment for engineers because many organizations place a high premium on the publicity they generate. It is an effective alternative to advertising.

In the broader field of technical writing, the work of engineers can be crucial to businesses and industries not only when they need to promote products and services but also when they need to communicate clearly to regulatory agencies, employees, and consumers. Such documents as Good Management Practices (GMP), ISO 9000 procedures, and health and safety policies have become the lifeblood of many industries. The ability of an organization to communicate these, and other, topics is vital to a company's competitive edge and long-term financial well-being.

The technical knowledge of the engineer is not only an advantage in preparing documentation to support the product and the process, but it is essential in defending the document, the product, and the process to many regulatory agencies. The basic technical understanding that engineers have makes it easier for them to produce the technical documents needed by the organization.

Entry-level salaries are not generally as high as those earned by engineers entering production or research and development, and advancement opportunities are not as numerous in this career field. However, there is a growing need for technical writers almost everywhere that scientific and engineering work is performed.

In some employment areas, an advanced degree in communications or journalism is advantageous for advancement. Therefore, it is advisable to take the Graduate Record Examination (GRE). It is usually required for admission to graduate study in a wide range of fields, including engineering, journalism, and communications. Because GRE scores are valid for five years, it is easier to take the exam at the end of your undergraduate studies rather than several years after graduation. Then, when you or your employer think that it would be good for your career advancement to enter a graduate program, you have the necessary test for admission already completed.

Additional Information

Society for Technical Communication, Inc.
901 N. Stuart St., Suite 904
Arlington, VA 22203-1822
stc.org

National Writers Union—National Office West
337 17th St., #101
Oakland, CA 94612
nwu.org

American Society of Indexers
10200 West 44th Ave., Suite 304
Wheat Ridge, CO 80033
asindexing.org

American Medical Writers Association
40 West Gude Dr., Suite 101
Rockville, MD 20850-1192
amwa.org

Council of Science Editors
c/o Drohan Management Group
11250 Roger Bacon Dr., Suite 8
Reston, VA 20190-5202
councilscienceeditors.org

Editorial Freelancers Association
71 West 23rd St., Suite 1910
New York, NY 10010
the-efa.org

International Webmasters Association
119 E Union St., Suite #F
Pasadena, CA 91103
iwanet.org

International Association of Business Communicators
One Hallidie Plaza, Suite 600
San Francisco, CA 94102-2818
iabc.com

National Association of Science Writers
P.O. Box 294
Greenlawn, NY 11740
nasw.org

Financial Services

The financial services industry has been providing an increasing number of opportunities for hands-on engineering, particularly for industrial engineers. However, there is also a growing number of engineers who decide to become commercial or investment bankers as well as financial traders.

Financial services organizations, such as Capital One and Chase Bank, are increasingly appearing on recruitment schedules at engineering schools. They are recruiting engineering graduates not only for technical positions but also for nontechnical, financial positions.

In the financial services industries, engineers can become involved in every aspect of the banking and investment business. This can include trading receivables, financing a plant expansion, and/or participating in the acquisition of a company.

Engineers in this field analyze industry trends in general and a customer's position within an industry specifically. They also assess the profitability of technology innovation, the marketability of that technology, the competition that will be faced, and the financial capacity of a client to compete in the marketplace.

Because of their strong quantitative skills, engineers often become involved in statistical and mathematical modeling for decision making within the financial services industries. Many engineers have chosen this career path because it offers interesting new opportunities for creative problem solving, such as determining creditworthiness, based on refined modeling of quantitative information.

Engineers in the financial services industry use knowledge of cost management, problem-solving skills, and analytical abilities to maximize resources. Therefore, there are many similarities between engineering skills and the requirements and demands of the financial-services profession. For example, banking is a demanding and fast-paced business. As a result of their education, engineers are accustomed to a heavy workload and to high levels of pressure. This makes them excellent candidates for positions in financial services. Some of the job functions in this area include:

Asset/investment management
Commercial banking/teller
Derivatives trading
Equities trading
Financial analyst
Financial consulting

Financial management
Fixed income trading
Insurance claims
Investment banking
Investment research
Loan officer
Risk management

It is important to keep in mind that the service sector is one of the fastest-growing sectors of the economy. Service-sector job opportunities are good, and salaries tend to be competitive with other traditional engineering areas. Advancement can be rapid for those who are able to contribute to the profitability of their clients and the organization.

Resources
The Daily Deal
The Economist
Financial Technology Network
Institutional Investor Newsletters
The New York Times
Red Herring
The Wall Street Journal
Web Finance

Advancement in the financial services sector can depend on your level of education. While advanced degrees in engineering (master's and Ph.D.) are valued in some areas of financial services, it will probably be necessary for you to complete a master's in business (M.B.A.) in order to advance. Therefore, it is advisable to take the General Management Aptitude Test (GMAT) for admission to business or management school when you finish your undergraduate degree. Check with your faculty advisor or the head of graduate studies for your school about the best time to take the GMAT. It's advisable to take it before leaving school, even if you are not sure that you will go to business school. GMAT scores are good for five years, and while you are in college you are in test-taking mode.

While the financial institution for which you work may already know the business school it wants you to attend, it is advisable to research various business schools. Many companies have selected business programs that fit their business philosophy and prepare people in a manner suited to the company's culture. If you are selected to attend such a business school you should still do your own research and develop a good understanding of what your company values in the curriculum of this particular institution.

If you have a choice of business schools, the research process is even more important. It should help you find a good fit between your educational needs and that of your company. All business schools are not alike. Each has its own mission and philosophy. You should know what that is and which one is best suited to meet your needs. It does not matter if your company selects or you select; it is always important for you to do your homework before making a decision about where you will apply to business school.

Additional Information

International Association of Financial Engineers
560 Lexington Ave., 9th Floor
New York, NY 10022
iafe.org

American Bankers Association
1120 Connecticut Ave. NW
Washington, DC 20036
aba.com

National Investment Banking Association
P.O. Box 6625
Athens, GA 30604
nibanet.org

Financial Planning Association
Denver office: 4100 E. Mississippi Ave., Suite 400
Denver, CO 80246-3053
District of Columbia office: 1600 K St. NW, Suite 201
Washington, DC 20006
fpanet.org

Legal Services

New technologies, such as genetic engineering and high-speed communication, are forcing the law to keep pace. Not only is technology influencing the practice of law, but the law is also influencing technology. Consequently, there is a growing need for lawyers who possess an engineering background in order to strengthen the level of communication between the legal field and the engineering field.

Lawyers who have been educated as engineers are in the best position to deal with the emerging issues of law and technology. An engineering background can give a lawyer a unique advantage. It can contribute to a more productive working relationship with an engineering client because the attorney possesses a fundamental understanding of the technical issues involved in the case.

According to the May, 2007, issue of Fortune magazine, the top five legal challenges for business leaders are:

1. Global compliance
2. Intellectual piracy
3. Product liability
4. Document retention
5. Employee lawsuits

All of these areas, not to mention patent law and environmental law, are good fits for someone with an engineering degree.

Patent law is an area of the law that draws heavily on engineering expertise. Patent law is not only of interest to industry but also to individual engineers who believe that they have made technological breakthroughs. Patents are important for one very simple reason: whoever holds a patent has the right to prevent others from using that technology for seventeen years. This can mean a competitive edge for an industry, and financial rewards for an individual.

The U.S. Patent and Trademark Office (PTO) is the federal government agency that grants patents. The PTO only grants a patent after intense scrutiny of the patent application. Therefore, the importance of a patent application cannot be emphasized too strongly. Accurate and thorough preparation is essential.

Individuals who prepare patent applications have to possess a basic legal knowledge as well as a high level of technical understanding. In addition, they must have excellent written and oral communication skills. Engineers can possess all of these characteristics.

While patent application documents are usually prepared by attorneys, engineers can prepare their own patent applications without holding a law degree. In addition, they can seek patents on behalf of others if they possess the appropriate technical credentials and have passed the PTO examination offered twice a year. Once they pass this exam, they become a patent agent.

Patent agents negotiate and draft patent agreements and prepare documents for filing and processing. You must be registered to practice with the U.S. Patent and Trademark Office and be familiar with standard concepts, practices, and procedures within a particular field. A certain degree of creativity and latitude is required to excel in this position, although patent agents report to a supervisor or manager.

Patent agents are limited in the services they can offer to their clients. For example, patent agents cannot file appeals of PTO decisions. They cannot draft and negotiate licensed use of patented inventions. Nor can they sue others who use inventions without licenses. As a result, patent agents usually go on to law school and become patent attorneys. With a law degree, they can command a higher salary, provide a wider range of services to their clients, and obtain malpractice insurance. These are benefits that patent agents do not enjoy.

Patent law is not the only legal area in which an engineering background is an advantage. With the impact of federal, state, and local regulations on technology and innovation, more attorneys are dealing with the highly technical regulations of such agencies as the Food and Drug Administration, the Environmental Protection Agency, the Occupational Safety and Health Administration, and others. This phenomena has resulted in new working relationships between the legal profession and the engineering profession.

In many industries, lawyers who specialize in government compliance work alongside staff and management engineers to ensure that products and processes meet current government regulations. For example, many medical device companies not only hire FDA compliance officers, but they also retain the services of law firms who specialize in FDA regulations and compliance. The requirements for clinical trials and Good Manufacturing Practices make the partnership between legal experts and engineering experts essential to doing business. The same is true for industries regulated by the EPA, that may also have engineers and lawyers working together to keep them in compliance. Obviously, a background in biomedical and environmental engineering gives lawyers in these areas a greater understanding of the issues involved in compliance.

Preparing for a Legal Career

While some engineers know that they want to pursue a legal career when they graduate from their undergraduate or graduate engineering program, others may not decide on this career path until later. As in the case of professional licensing, it is always good to take the prerequisite examination for admission to law school at the time of graduation. The Law School Admission Test (LSAT) is offered throughout the year (lsat-center.com). The scores from this exam, like others of its kind, are good for five years. Taking the exam when your test-taking skills are at their peak is strongly advised.

According to the American Bar Association, there were 196 accredited law schools in 2007. All but one of those schools grant the first degree in law (the J.D. degree); the other ABA-approved school is the U.S. Army Judge Advocate General's School. It offers an officer's resident graduate course, which is a specialized program beyond the first degree in law. For a complete list of accredited law schools, go to abanet.org/legaled/approvedlawschools/approved.html. Research and identify the law schools that provide the best legal education in the area of the law in which you are interested. Identify the law firms that routinely recruit from those law schools. Are these the types of firms you would be interested in working for after graduation? If so, these are the schools that will open the most doors for you upon graduation.

What to Expect in Law School. Your legal education will build on a set of core skills and values identified by the American Bar Association. These are:

- Analytic/problem-solving skills
- Critical reading
- Writing skills
- Oral communication/listening abilities
- General research skills
- Task organization/management skills
- Public service and promotion of justice

These map very well to the engineering skills and values that you have learned in your engineering education.

During your first year of law school, you will usually take courses in constitutional law, contracts, property law, torts, civil procedure, and legal writing. These are subjects that all lawyers must know to practice law. After the first year of law school, you can usually take courses in special legal areas such as environmental, patent, labor, or corporate law. An important part of your legal education is the practical experience you gain through school-sponsored legal clinic activities; moot court competitions; practice trials; and research and writing for the school's law journal. You can also gain experience working in legal aid clinics; on legislative committee staffs; and clerking in law firms, government agencies, and corporate legal departments and the judicial system.

Once you have completed law school, you must become licensed, or be admitted to the bar, in the state or states where you plan to practice law. All states require admission to the bar, which means you must pass an examination. Most states also require that you pass a separate exam on ethics. There is an exception. Federal courts and agencies set their own qualifications for those practicing before or in them.

Once you are licensed and admitted to the bar, it will be necessary to stay up to date through continuing legal education. It will be important to know the requirements for continued licensure in your state (abanet.org/bar serv/stlobar.html).

While there are many career paths for newly graduated attorneys, many start as associates in law firms. In this position, they support and work with experienced lawyers. After several years, you can be eligible to be considered for partnership in your firm. The process of becoming a partner is similar to the tenure process for engineers who have chosen the academic career path. The quality of your work as a lawyer is closely evaluated by the partners and a decision is made to offer you partnership or not.

In addition to joining a law firm, you might decide to form your own company. Another option is to join the office of the legal counsel for a corporation. Because of their strong writing and oral communication skills, some attorneys go into reporting and broadcasting. There's a broad career path available to lawyers, particularly lawyers with a background in engineering.

Additional Information

American Bar Association
321 N. Clark St.
Chicago, IL 60610
abanet.org

American Intellectual Property Law Association
241 18th St. South, Suite 700
Arlington, VA 22202
aipla.org

Global Compliance
13950 Ballantyne Corporate Place, Suite 300
Charlotte, NC 28277
globalcompliance.com/associations.html

International Bar Association
10th Floor, 1 Stephen St.
London W1T 1AT, United Kingdom
ibanet.org

Medical Services

Each year an increasing number of engineering majors apply to and are admitted to medical school. The combination of an engineering and a medical education gives these individuals an opportunity to apply both their knowledge of medicine and their knowledge of technology in this new age of health care. Recent technological advances in rehabilitation, orthopedics, and surgery have been the result not only of collaboration between engineers and doctors but also of the expertise of doctor/engineers, who are able to work and communicate in both worlds.

Medical students with engineering backgrounds have specialized in all of the medical disciplines, with many pursuing specialties such as orthopedics, ophthalmology, neurology, and surgery. The relationship of these medical areas to mechanics, optics, and instrumentation is a good extension of these students' engineering education. Indeed, the technological breakthroughs in these particular areas illustrate the partnership between engineering and medicine and the need for engineering expertise in these areas.

Engineering majors who plan to go on to medical school after graduation must take particular care in planning their undergraduate experience. First, they must make sure that they use their elective credits wisely. It is necessary for them to take a number of courses outside of engineering. These courses include the undergraduate organic chemistry series, as well as the basic biology series with the laboratory section. In addition, it is strongly advised that engineers planning to go to medical school take additional course work in English and other humanities.

While medical admissions committees expect engineering applicants to demonstrate strong problem-solving skills and good hands-on abilities, they can also hold a prejudice that engineers do not have good communication skills. This means that the admissions committee will need to see that an engineering applicant has addressed this potential deficit through course selection and extracurricular activities that reflect strong oral and written communication skills.

For engineers planning to attend medical school, it is advisable to take public speaking and writing courses. Their performance in these classes will be a demonstration of good communication skills. Likewise, involvement in extracurricular activities such as student government, theater, forensic programs, Toastmasters clubs, and so on can also demonstrate strong skills in this area. Any extracurricular activity that demonstrates strong leadership is also extremely helpful.

Because medical schools tend to prefer applicants who demonstrate a good understanding of the profession, it is strongly advised that engineering majors planning to study medicine gain experience related to the medical profession. Participation in the cooperative education program, internship programs, or volunteer experience in medical settings is important.

During the spring term of the junior year or the fall term of the senior year, engineering majors who are thinking about and preparing for medical school should take the Medical College Aptitude Test (MCAT). It is required for admission to all medical schools in the United States, and the scores are good for five years. Therefore, even if you are uncertain as to whether or not you will be applying to medical school right after graduation, it is a very good idea to take this exam before completing your undergraduate studies.

Admission to medical school is highly competitive. Your engineering degree might give you an advantage, but it is not a guarantee of admission. You will still need to demonstrate exemplary academic achievement, leadership, communication skills, and a good understanding of what the profession will require. In years past, admission to medical school was primarily given to recent undergraduates with no real-world experience. Today it is not uncommon for people with several years of work experience in industry to pursue a medical career. Therefore, if you have not decided definitely that medicine is a career path you want to pursue, you have time to make that decision. However, your undergraduate record should still reflect your commitment to the life sciences, communications, and leadership.

A medical education is lengthy and involves four years of medical school, three to seven years of residency, and one to three years in a subspecialty fellowship. Medical school consists of preclinical and clinical parts.

A residency program is more professional training. The first year of residency is also known as an internship. Training at this level is done under the close supervision of senior physicians. The length of a residency depends on the specialty. Some require three years and others, like surgery, require five or more years. A fellowship is for physicians who want to become highly specialized in fields like cardiology, radiology or nuclear medicine, internal medicine, and so on.

After completing this extensive education, a doctor must obtain a license to practice medicine from the state where he or she plans to practice. This is accomplished by completing a series of exams and a minimum number of years of graduate medical education.

Physicians can also choose to become board certified. Certification ensures that doctors have been tested on knowledge, skills, and experience in a specialty. Most certifications must be renewed after six to ten years, depending on the specialty. In addition, doctors must continue to receive credits for continuing medical education to ensure that knowledge and skills remain current. These requirements vary by state, by professional organizations, and by hospital medical staff organizations.

Additional Information

Association of American Medical Colleges
2450 N St. NW
Washington, DC 20037-1126
aamc.org

American Medical Association
515 N. State St.
Chicago, IL 60610
ama-assn.org

American Medical College Application Service (AMCAS®)
P.O. Box 57326
Washington, DC 20037
aamc.org/students/amcas/start.htm

Medical College Admission Test (MCAT) Website
aamc.org/students/mcat/start.htm

Appendix

State Examining Boards

Source: National Council of Examiners for Engineering and Surveying (nceesorg/licensure/licensing_boards)

Alabama

State Board of Licensure for Professional Engineers and Surveyors
The RSA Union
100 N. Union St., Ste 382
Montgomery, AL 36104-3762

Alaska

State Board of Registration for Architects, Engineers, and Land Surveyors
P.O. Box 110806
Juneau, AK 99811-0806

Arizona

State Board of Technical Registration
1110 W. Washington St., Suite 240
Phoenix, AZ 85007

Arkansas

State Board of Registration for Professional Engineers and Land
  Surveyors
P.O. Box 3750
Little Rock, AR 72203

California

Board of Registration for Professional Engineers and
  Land Surveyors
2535 Capitol Oaks Dr., Ste 300
Sacramento, CA 95833-2944

Colorado

State Board of Registration for Professional Engineers and Professional
  Land Surveyors
1560 Broadway, Ste 1350
Denver, CO 80202

Connecticut

State Board of Examiners for Professional Engineers and Land
  Surveyors
The State Office Bldg, Rm 110
165 Capitol Ave.
Hartford, CT 06106-1630

Delaware

Delaware Association of Professional Engineers
56 W. Main St., Ste 208,
  Plaza 273
Christiana, DE 19702

State Board of Registration for Professional Land Surveyors
Cannon Bldg, 861 Silver Lake, Suite 203
Dover, DE 19904

District of Columbia

Board of Registration for Professional Engineers
941 N. Capitol St. NE, Suite 7200
Washington, DC 20002

Florida

Board of Professional Engineers
2507 Callaway Rd., Suite 200
Tallahassee, FL 32303

Board of Professional Surveyors and Mappers
1940 N. Monroe St.
Tallahassee, FL 32399-0756

Georgia

State Board of Registration for Professional Engineers and Land
    Surveyors
237 Coliseum Dr.
Macon, GA 31217-3858

Guam

Guam Board of Registration for Professional Engineers, Architects and
    Land Surveyors
Government of Guam
EW Business Center
718 N. Marine Dr., Unit D, Ste 308
Upper Tumon, GU 96913

Hawaii

Board of Registration of Professional Engineers, Architects, Surveyors and Landscape Architects
P.O. Box 3469
Honolulu, HI 96801

Idaho

Board of Professional Engineers and Professional Land Surveyors
5535 West Overland Rd.
Boise, ID 83705

Illinois

Department of Professional Regulation Land Surveyors Board
320 W. Washington St., 3rd Fl
Springfield, IL 62786

Department of Professional Regulation State Board of Professional Engineers
320 W. Washington St., 3rd Fl
Springfield, IL 62786

Department of Professional Regulation Structural Engineering Board
320 W. Washington St., 3rd Fl
Springfield, IL 62786

Indiana

State Board of Registration for Professional Engineers
402 W. Washington St., Room W072
Indianapolis, IN 46204

State Board of Registration for Professional Land Surveyors
402 W. Washington Street, Room W072
Indianapolis, IN 46204

Iowa

Engineering and Land Surveying Examining Board
1920 SE Hulsizer Rd.
Ankeny, IA 50021

Kansas

State Board of Technical Professions
Landon State Office Bldg.
900 Jackson, Ste 507
Topeka, KS 66612-1257

Kentucky

**State Board of Licensure for Professional Engineers and
    Land Surveyors**
Kentucky Engineering Center
160 Democrat Dr.
Frankfort, KY 40601

Louisiana

Louisiana Professional Engineering and Land Surveying Board
9643 Brookline Ave., Ste 121
Baton Rouge, LA 70809-1443

Maine

State Board of Licensure for Professional Land Surveyors
35 State House Station
Augusta, ME 04333-0035

State Board of Registration for Professional Engineers
92 State House Station
Augusta, ME 04333-0092

Maryland

State Board for Professional Engineers
500 N. Calvert St., Rm 308
Baltimore, MD 21202-3651

State Board for Professional Land Surveyors
500 N. Calvert St., Rm 308
Baltimore, MD 21202-3651

Massachusetts

Board of Registration of Professional Engineers and Professional Land
  Surveyors
Division of Registration
239 Causeway St.
Boston, MA 02114

Michigan

Department of Consumer and Industry Services Board of Professional
  Engineers
P.O. Box 30018
Lansing, MI 48909

Board of Professional Surveyors
P.O. Box 30018
Lansing, MI 48909

Minnesota

State Board of Architecture, Engineering Land Surveying, Landscape
  Architecture, Geoscience, and Interior Design
The Golden Rule Bldg., Ste 160
85 E. Seventh Pl.
St. Paul, MN 55101-2113

Mississippi

State Board of Registration for Professional Engineers and Land
Surveyors
The Robert E Lee Bldg
239 N. Lamar, Ste 501
Jackson, MS 39205

Missouri

Board for Architects, Professional Engineers and
Land Surveyors
3605 Missouri Blvd., Ste 380
P.O. Box 184
Jefferson City, MO 65102

Montana

Board of Professional Engineers and
Land Surveyors
Dept. of Commerce
P.O. Box 200513
301 S Park Ave., 4th Fl
Helena, MT 59620-0513

Nebraska

Board of Engineers and Architects
215 Centennial Mall South,
Suite 400
P.O. Box 95165
Lincoln, NE 68509

Board of Examiners for Land Surveyors
555 N. Cotner Blvd., Lower Level
Lincoln, NE 68505

Nevada

State Board of Professional Engineers and Land Surveyors
1755 E. Plumb Ln., Ste 135
Reno, NV 89502

New Hampshire

Board of Professional Engineers
57 Regional Dr.
Concord, NH 03301

State Board of Licensure for Land Surveyors
57 Regional Dr.
Concord, NH 03301

New Jersey

State Board of Professional Engineers and Land Surveyors
124 Halsey St., 3rd Fl
Newark, NJ 07102

New Mexico

Board of Registration for Professional Engineers and Surveyors
Department of Registration and Licensing
4001 Office Court Dr., Suite 903
Santa Fe, NM 87507

New York

State Board for Engineering and Land Surveying
State Education Bldg
2nd Fl Mezzanine East-Wing
89 Washington Ave.
Albany, NY 12234-1000

North Carolina

Board of Examiners for Engineers and Surveyors
4601 Six Forks Rd., Suite 310
Raleigh, NC 27609

North Dakota

State Board of Registration for Professional Engineers and Land
    Surveyors
723 West Memorial Highway
Bismarck, ND 58504

Northern Mariana Islands

Board of Professional Licensing
Commonwealth of Northern Mariana Islands
P.O. Box 502078
Saipan, Northern Mariana Islands 96950

Ohio

State Board of Registration for Professional Engineers
    and Surveyors
77 South High St.,
    Room 1698
Columbus, OH 43215-6108

Oklahoma

State Board of Registration for Professional Engineers and Land
    Surveyors
Oklahoma Engineering Center,
    Room 120
201 NE 27th St.
Oklahoma City, OK 73105

Oregon

State Board of Examiners for Engineering and
  Land Surveying
670 Hawthorne Ave. SE,
  Suite 220
Salem, OR 97301

Pennsylvania

State Registration Board for Professional Engineers, Land Surveyors,
  and Geologists
P.O. Box 2649
Harrisburg, PN 17105-2649

Puerto Rico

Board of Examiners of Engineers, Architects,
and Surveyors
151 Fortaleza St.
Marshall Bldg., 3rd Fl
San Juan, PR 00901-3271

Rhode Island

State Board of Registration for Professional Engineers
State Office Bldg.
1 Capitol Hill,
  2nd Fl
Providence, RI 02908

Board of Registration for Professional
  Land Surveyors
State Office Bldg.
1 Capitol Hill, 2nd Fl
Providence, RI 02908

South Carolina

State Board of Registration for Professional Engineers and Land Surveyors
110 Centerview Dr.
Kingstree Bldg., Suite 201
P.O. Box 11597
Columbia, SC 29210-1597

South Dakota

Board of Technical Professions
2040 W. Main St., Ste 304
Rapid City, SD 57702-2447

Tennessee

State Board of Architectural and Engineering Examiners
Department of Commerce and Insurance
500 James Robertson Pkwy., 3rd Fl
Nashville, TN 37243

State Board of Examiners for Land Surveyors
500 James Robertson Pkwy., 2nd Fl
Nashville, TN 37243-1146

Texas

Board of Professional Engineers
1917 Interstate Highway 35 S.
Austin, TX 78741

State Board of Land Surveying
12100 Park 35 Circle
Building A, MC-230, Suite 156
Austin, TX 78753

Utah

**Utah Professional Engineers and Professional Land
Surveyors Board**
160 E. 300 South
Box 146741
Salt Lake City, UT 84114-6741

Vermont

Board of Land Surveyors
Secretary of State
81 River St., Heritage Building
Montpelier, VT 05609

Board of Professional Engineering
Office of Professional Regulation
26 Terrace St., Drawer 09
Montpelier, VT 05609-1101

Virginia

**Board of Architects, Professional Engineers, Land Surveyors, and
Landscape Architects**
Department of Professional and Occupational Regulation
3600 W. Broad St.
Richmond, VA 23230-4917

Virgin Islands

Board for Architects, Engineers and Land Surveyors
Dept of Licensing and Consumer Affairs
Golden Rock Shopping Center
Christiansted, St. Croix
Virgin Islands 00820

Washington

State Board of Registration for Professional Engineers and Land
   Surveyors
405 Black Lake Blvd. SW
Olympia, WA 98502

West Virginia

State Board of Examiners of Land Surveyors
2298 Sutton Ln.
Flatwoods, WV 26621

State Board of Registration for Professional Engineers
300 Capital St., Suite 910
Charleston, WV 25301

Wisconsin

Examining Board of Architects, Landscape Architects, Geologists,
   Professional Engineers, Designers, and Land Surveyors
1400 E. Washington Ave.
Madison, WI 53703-8935

Wyoming

State Board of Registration for Professional Engineers and Professional
   Land Surveyors
6920 Yellowtail Dr., Suite 100
Cheyenne, WY 82002

Index

About the Author

Dr. Geraldine Garner is the President of Science and Technology Career Strategies, Inc. (STCS, Inc.), which works with companies concerned with retaining key engineering, scientific, and IT/computer talent. Garner began her career as a co-op coordinator for mechanical and biomedical engineering students at Virginia Tech. Later she became associate dean and associate professor of the Walter P. Murphy Cooperative Engineering Education Program in the Robert R. McCormick School of Engineering at Northwestern University. She has taught graduate and undergraduate courses in career development theory at Northwestern University and Virginia Commonwealth University. In addition to her many academic honors, she is widely published in the area of engineering career development.

Garner holds a doctorate in career counseling from Virginia Tech and a bachelor's and master's degrees from The College of William and Mary. She is the author of a variety of books, articles, and papers and has received numerous honors for her work with engineers' career development.